Do you remember our fishing expedition in company with congress man Van Allen to the little lake a few miles from Kinderhook; and John Moore the vagabond admiral of the lake who sat crouched in a heap in the middle of his canoe in the centre of the lake, with fishing rods stretching out in every direction like the long legs of a spider. And do you remember our piratical prank, when we made up by for our own bad luck in fishing by plundering plundering his canoe of its fish when we found it adrift. and do you remember how John Moore came splashing along the marsh on the opposite border of the lake, roaring at us, and how we finished our prolick by driving off and leaving the congress man to John Moores mercy; tickling ourselves with the idea of his being scalped at least. ah well aday friend Merwin; these were the days of our youth and folly, I trust we have grown wiser and better since then; we certainly have grown older. I dont think we would rob John Moores fishing canoe now. By the way that same and the anecdotes you told of him, John Moore, gave me the idea of a vagabond character, Dirk Schuyler, in my Knickerbocker history of New York, which I was then writing.

Part of a Letter from Irving to Merwin

This book is marketed both as *The Forgotten Legend of Sleepy Hollow* and *Legend of Sleepy Hollow, Rip Van Winkle, President Van Buren and Brom.*

Library of Congress Cataloging in Publication Data

Welles, E. R.
  Legend of Sleepy Hollow, Rip Van Winkle, President Van Buren, and Brom, a book telling their interrelations for all ages.

  Published also under the title: The Forgotten Legend of Sleepy Hollow.
  Includes the texts of Washington Irving's Legend of Sleepy Hollow and Rip Van Winkle.
  Includes bibliographical references.
  1. Irving, Washington, 1783–1859, in fiction, drama, poetry, etc.
I. Evans, J. P. II. Irving, Washington, 1783–1859. Legend of Sleepy Hollow. 1984. III. Irving, Washington, 1783–1859. Rip Van Winkle. 1984. IV. Title.
PS3573.E4572F6   1984   813'.54   84-878
ISBN 0-913692-10-7

Library of Congress Cataloging in Publication Data

Welles, E. R.
  The Forgotten Legend of Sleepy Hollow.
  Includes the texts of Washington Irving's Legend of Sleepy Hollow and Rip Van Winkle.
  Includes bibliographical references.
  1. Irving, Washington, 1783–1859, in fiction, drama, poetry, etc.
I. Evans, J. P. II. Irving, Washington, 1783–1859. Legend of Sleepy Hollow. 1984. III. Irving, Washington, 1783–1859. Rip Van Winkle. 1984. IV. Title.
PS3573.E4572F6   1984b   813'.54   84-7145
ISBN 0-913692-12-3

The Forgotten Legend of Sleepy Hollow

now also called:

Legend of Sleepy Hollow, Rip Van Winkle, President Van Buren And BROM

"A book telling their interrelations for all ages"

E.R. WELLES, III and J.P. EVANS

LEARNING INCORPORATED
MANSET, MAINE 04656

Printed in the United States of America.

As: *The Forgotten Legend of Sleepy Hollow:*
  ISBN: 0-913692-12-3 (Paperback)

As: *Legend of Sleepy Hollow, Rip Van Winkle,*
  President van Buren and Brom:
  ISBN 0-913692-10-7

Cover of *Legend of Sleepy Hollow, Rip Van Winkle, President Van Buren and Brom* designed by:
  Dale Ingrid Swensson
  Southwest Harbor, Maine

Typeset by: Beech Hill Enterprises, Inc.
  Southwest Harbor, Maine

Dedication

by E.R. Welles, III, to all persons who helped, and especially my parents; my grandparents, Mr. and Mrs. William Beekman van Alstyne; my teachers, Loretta Ellen Brady (history and research) and Amey Steere (spelling and reading); my Aunt Mary Welles; my Aunt Elizabeth Kellogg van Alstyne; my wife; and my friends, Mr. and Mrs. Robert Davidson.

Thanks

is acknowledged to the Kinderhook (New York) Public Library for its helpful information about Washington Irving; the Columbia County (New York) Historical Society Librarian, Louise Hardenbrook, for information about the Merwin family; Felex O.C. Darley for his 1849 design and etching of Rip van Winkle and the mysterious bowlers; Kinderhook's Ichabod Crane School's Superintendent, Leverett Mansfield for playing Ichabod Crane in 1965; former Kinderhook Mayor Abram van Alstyne for playing the Headless Horsemen in 1965; and the author of *A History of Old Kinderhook,* Edward A. Collier, D.D., for his 1914 book's informative and illustrative assistance.

Preface

THE STORY WHICH FOLLOWS is based on the belief of a number of persons, who have done extensive research into the matter, that Washington Irving received inspiration for "The Legend of Sleepy Hollow," as well as for part of his equally well-known and beloved story "Rip van Winkle," while staying in Kinderhook, New York, and that the locale of the former tale is actually that of Kinderhook rather than Tarrytown, as is popularly believed. This story too, then, is a legend of a sleepy hollow.

The boy Brom and Gram in the story are fictional. On the other hand, Jesse Merwin, Jane van Dyck, and Abram van Alstyne all once actually lived in Kinderhook, and Merwin's Pond, Merwin's schoolhouse, and the van Alen homestead, and President Martin van Buren's home, Lindenwald, are actual places. The tale the old man tells Brom concerning the relationship of these people and places to Washington Irving's stories is based on historical fact contained in the brief sketch of Irving which appears at the end of the book.

As to whether the old man and his dog, Wolf, the bowlers in the Catskill Mountains, and the Headless Horseman are fact or fiction, it is left to the reader to decide for himself.

E.R.W., III, and J.P.E.
Manset, Maine
1973

1984 Preface: Since this work was first published it has been suggested that we alter the original title in order to reach a wider audience of interested persons. Consequently we've decided to publish this work under both the original title and the altered one.

Further, since first publication, the Martin van Buren National Historic Site has been established at Lindenwald by act of the Congress and President of the USA. Bruce Stewart, first National Park Service superintendent of the Site, and his associates have asked for the historic references used to establish the factual aspects of this work. We have decided to share these references with all of our readers as well as to include the original texts of Irving's *Legend of Sleepy Hollow* and *Rip van Winkle* since these two stories have so often been altered in various publications and movies.

Table of Contents

Chapter 1

The Pond

ON THAT DAY, as Brom raced down the old country road, he had never felt so happy and free. True, his school bookbag, made of faded green cloth, was slung over his shoulder like a small sea bag. Now it was empty of books and held only his lunch and an extra sweater. He had come just last night from the city to his grandmother's farm and could hardly believe a fair amount of time was to be his to enjoy. Though he had been to the farm before, this was to be his first stay without his parents, and Gram had packed lunch for him and sent him off to explore.

Beyond the fields on both sides of the road there were woods he had never been into, but he did not stop to inspect them, since he was anxious to get to the unknown territory that lay on the other side of the hill ahead of him. When he approached the top of the ridge he came to a fork in the road. Pausing to decide which way he should go, Brom turned and looked back. There to the west, beyond the woods and fields he had passed, he could see the broad expanse of the Hudson River Valley. In the distance, behind low rolling hills, stretched a range of mountains which Gram had told him were the Catskills. These were the same mountains he had seen from his

window when he'd jumped out of bed early that morning. Silhouetted against the sky, they had looked to Brom like an old man with a long beard, lying fast asleep on his back. Looking now, he could no longer see the old man, for the tops of the mountains were hidden by clouds.

Brom decided to take the left fork and was glad he had done so, for soon he came upon a small pond in a hollow of the hill. As he gazed across the water, he caught his breath. There, sitting at the end of a broken down dam at the pond's outlet, was an old man with a long white beard who was surely the old man of the mountains. The road skirted the edge of the pond. As Brom came closer he could see that the old man was clad in a pair of very ragged, old-fashioned breeches, like those worn by Brom's Dutch ancestors in pictures Gram had at the farm. The old man held a long fishing pole in his hands and was gazing intently at the spot where he hoped the fish would rise. All of a sudden Brom turned to run, for out of the grass by the dam there sprang a big gray dog, that growled at the approaching boy. Looking up and seeing no one but Brom, the old man cried "Down, Wolf!" and the dog went back to his master. As Brom hesitated, the old man smiled and motioned to him to come sit beside him. Brom saw then that his blue eyes were twinkling and he knew in an instant that they would be friends.

For a while they sat in silence as the old man returned to his fishing. Brom watched with curiosity mixed with envy,

Merwin's Lake, Irving's Fishing Resort

wishing that he, too, might be fishing. The old man must have read his thoughts, for after a bit he turned to Brom and asked, "Would you like me to cut you a pole?"

Brom nodded. He could hardly contain his delight as the old man pulled a knife from his leather belt and cut off a branch of a maple sapling growing nearby. After searching about for some string to tie to the end of the branch and to which he attached a fishhook, he took a worm from the can by his side, baited the hook, and handed the rod to Brom.

Though the fish did not seem to be biting that day, the two fishermen were content. Soaking up the sun like turtles which have just emerged from their winter quarters, they enjoyed the peace surrounding them. For the most part, the surface of the pond was smooth, but once in a while a little puff of wind from the southwest would ruffle the water and with it bring the scent of pine trees from the nearby hillside.

Since by now it was well past noon, the birds were quiet, though a redwing would sometimes rise from the cattails in the marsh opposite them. But for the blackbird's song or an occasional croak of a frog, all was still, and the fishermen soon became drowsy and were tempted to join the dog sleeping beside them. But Brom had had breakfast a long while ago and he decided it was high time to take out the lunch from his book-bag. Gram had provided him with ample supplies: sandwiches, two huge pieces of cake, and a couple of oranges, as well as a thermos of milk. So there was more than enough

The "Half Moon" in Kinderhook Waters
From a photograph

is called Kinderhook, since that is the Dutch for 'Children's Corner,' and the name Hudson marked on his chart.[1] In fact, for this reason Kinderhook can be considered the oldest continuously used white man's name for a place in the State of New York. How would you feel if you had ancestors who had lived in one of the first Dutch settlements in this country?"

"But I have!" Brom cried out. "I'm descended from the original settlers of Kinderhook." Jumping up in excitement, he looked so proud that the old man could not help but laugh.

As they were talking, dark clouds had been gathering and both knew it was time to go, or Brom would not reach the farm before the storm broke. Fishing poles in hand, the two trudged together to the top of the hill with Wolf trotting on before them. When they came to the fork in the road the old man and his dog turned left, while Brom went the other way which led to Gram's farm. He got back just as the rain was beginning to fall. To him the return journey had taken no time at all, for his head had been full of thoughts of strange bearded men high up in the distant mountains.

Chapter 2

Brom's Dream

W HEN BROM WENT TO BED that night it was rain-
ing hard and the thunder and lightning were still close
at hand. As he drifted off to sleep after his day out-
doors, he dreamt he was far away climbing up a mountain.
Beside him was a tall, thin man with a large dog. Though the
man had no beard and was younger than the old man the boy
had met at the pond, he did look very much like him and wore
the same kind of breeches. The dog resembled Wolf, though
he, too, was younger. Gone was the fishing pole and in its place
Brom's companion carried a gun like the ancient fowling-piece
hanging above Gram's fireplace.

As they climbed higher, the trail became steeper and more
rocky. Every once in a while they could hear rumbling noises
coming from a ravine ahead of them. Suddenly they found
themselves in a hollow in the ravine and there, in his dream,
Brom saw the same strange bearded man he had been thinking about on his way home from the pond. They looked grim,
not at all as if they were enjoying their game of bowling on
a long level strip in the hollow. There was no sound except
the thundering peals of the bowling balls as they rolled down
the strip and crashed into the pins standing erect at the other

end. Clad in jerkins or doublets and big heavy breeches, these men looked very peculiar to Brom, far more so than his climbing companion.

Many of the bowlers were short, with broad faces and little eyes. All had beards, some grizzled and gray, some red, while others were blonde in color. Long knives were stuck in their belts and their swarthy complexions suggested they had just come from a long sea voyage. One of them, who appeared as the leader, wore a high hat with a white feather sticking out from its crown. As Brom watched in amazement, several of the men would at times break off from their game to fill large mugs with some sort of drink from a wooden keg nearby, but other than that they kept to their bowling. Brom turned to ask his companion if the men were real, and if so, could they be Hendrick Hudson and his crew, but just at that moment there was a flash of lightning so bright that it blinded him.

When the lightning was gone, Brom saw that the bowlers had vanished, as well as the man with his dog, and, in his dream, Brom found himself no longer on the mountainside, but instead walking along a dark lonely road. Suddenly there were noises like thunder but this time they sounded as if they were horses' hooves pounding along the road beside him. As the sounds grew louder, Brom jumped aside, for he realized the galloping horses were nearly upon him.

Brom could just make out two riders, side by side. One seemed to be thin and lanky and was having great difficulty keeping his seat as he swayed back and forth in the saddle. The other loomed up huge against the trees. He was cloaked and rode a black steed, gigantic in contrast to the skinny horse of his companion. As they passed by, the lightning flashed again and Brom thought he had never seen such a look of fright as that on the thin man's face. Even more terrifying, however, was what Brom saw on the big black horse. His rider sat tall

and straight, but where there should have been a head on his shoulders, there was none. Instead, the head, round like a pumpkin, was propped up on the saddle before him, steadied by his hand.

When the sounds of horses' hooves had faded and the riders vanished into the night, Brom continued walking along the road. His heart thumped, when, as he passed an old church-yard, he heard something coming toward him. It was the same big black horse, returning, but which now had slowed to a walk. Although the man still wore a cloak on his back, Brom could see that his head was where it should be. As the horse came nearer, he saw too that the rider was laughing, as if at some huge joke. Another flash of lightning revealed his whole face and Brom was startled at the likeness to his own.

Just then there was a loud crackling noise, too sharp to be thunder, and Brom woke up with a start. A limb of the old apple tree outside his window was lying on the sill. Brom supposed it must have been broken off by the wind, but he didn't lie there long wondering about it, for the sun was now shining and it was time to get up.

Chapter 3

The Old Man's Story

B ROM DIDN'T TELL Gram of his dream for he was afraid she would think he was sick and not let him go back that day to the pond which he wanted to do more than anything else in the world. He had a feeling that the old man might be able to explain the dream to him and he could hardly wait to be off. As he hurried through breakfast he asked Gram if he could go exploring again. She was pleased to see him so full of life and since the day was a nice one, Gram packed up a lunch and sent him on his way.

This time Brom took his fishing pole made from the maple sapling, as well as the lunch in his book-bag, and it wasn't long before he came to the pond. As he had hoped, the old man was there, fishing from the dam, with Wolf at his side. Today the dog wagged his tail as the boy came near, hoping, perhaps, that Brom would give him a piece of cake as he had done yesterday. Brom patted Wolf on the head and settled himself beside the old man. Soon he began to tell him of dreaming about going up into the mountains and seeing the strange bearded men. As he talked, Brom noticed the same far away look in the old man's eyes which had been there the day before when they had spoken of Hendrick Hudson and his crew bowling in the Cat-

Washington Irving
From an etching by Thomas Johnson

skills. When he had finished that part of his tale, the old man nodded, but did not seem surprised at what Brom had told him.

"You dreamed of Rip van Winkle," he said.

"Who was he?" Brom asked, though he thought he'd heard Gram mention the name once before.

The old man's eyes twinkled in amusement. "I know very well and I'll tell you."

He paused as if to get his breath and then went on, "In 1783 a famous American writer named Washington Irving was born. He wrote many books during his lifetime, but perhaps he is best remembered for his story, 'Rip van Winkle,' about a man who lived in a village at the foot of the Catskills. Rip would often take his dog and his gun and go up into the mountains to hunt, for he was hen-pecked by a nagging wife and wished to escape. On one of these trips he came upon the men bowling just as you've described them. After partaking of the drink in their wooden keg, Rip fell fast asleep. When he awoke he found that the dog had disappeared and his freshly oiled gun was all rusty, which puzzled him very much. Making his way back to the village, he discovered all had changed. Many of the familiar houses were gone, as well as his old friends. The people he met he didn't know, nor did they recognize him in his old-fashioned breeches, all ragged and torn."

At mention of the breeches, Brom was reminded of those the old man wore and of how much he and Brom's climbing companion of the dream resembled each other. The old man smiled as if he guessed what the boy was thinking about, but he continued on.

"The villagers challenged this stranger. Rip claimed he was a loyal subject of King George, but they called him a spy, since America was no longer governed by England, and had become the United States.

"Finally, an old woman recognized Rip behind his long gray beard and asked him where he had been the past twenty years. Rip realized then that his sleep had lasted more than one night and that a Revolutionary War had been fought and a new country formed while he had been sleeping. Many considered him out of his mind when they heard his tale of the bowling. But the story of Rip van Winkle ended happily for he was reunited with his son and daughter and eventually accepted by the villagers as one of their most respected patriarchs."

Brom was amazed that what he had dreamt was part of a story and he wondered if the rest of his dream were, too. It was time now for lunch. As they ate, giving Wolf some of the cake, Brom told the old man about the headless horseman and his companion rider.

Again the old man showed no surprise. "Yes, that was part of another well known tale Washington Irving wrote, 'The Legend of Sleepy Hollow,' about a schoolmaster named Ichabod Crane, the lanky and frightened man you saw, who could barely stick to his galloping horse."

"Tell me the story," Brom begged, for he wanted to know who the other rider had been.

The old man was pleased and went on. "Ichabod Crane had come from Connecticut to teach in a quiet little valley near the Hudson River, known to its Dutch inhabitants as Sleepy Hollow. According to Washington Irving, there were many legends connected with this hollow, among them a story of a Hessian whose head had been shot off in the Revolutionary War and whose ghost now rode at night in search of the missing head."

The boy shivered, for the memory of his dream was fresh in his mind. "What's a Hessian?" he asked.

"A German trooper from Hesse; some of them fought in the war on the British side under General Burgoyne,"[2] the old man explained, then continued with the story.

"Not too long after he had come to the valley, Ichabod fell in love with Katrina van Tassel, the daughter of a prosperous Dutch farmer. One dark night, when riding home from a party at the van Tassel's farm, he was terrified by a headless horseman who rode up beside him on a black horse. Ichabod tried to escape, but the horseman stuck close beside him and they rode along together, just as you saw them in your dream. After that night the schoolmaster was never seen again in Sleepy Hollow, though the old horse he had borrowed returned, saddleless, to his master. The saddle was later found by the roadside, and farther on, near a brook, lay Ichabod's hat together with pieces of a broken pumpkin.

"No one ever knew whether Ichabod had indeed ridden with the ghost of the Hessian, or whether he had had a trick played upon him by his rival for Katrina's favors, Abram van Brunt, better known as 'Brom Bones,' since 'Brom' is the Dutch for 'Abram' and he was such a big-boned fellow. So you see, the headless horseman in your dream could have been the Hessian's ghost or he could have been Brom Bones, the rider you saw returning on the big black horse."

As the old man paused, the boy burst out, "Why, Brom's MY name, and, you know, that last rider, well, he looked just

Jesse Merwin
(Ichabod Crane)
From an old photograph

like ME! Don't you think that's strange?"

"No; there is an explanation for it. In fact, it is believed that much of what Washington Irving put into these tales can be traced to this region in which you have such deep family roots."

"What do you mean?" Brom asked.

"I'll try to explain," the old man said. "Listen patiently, for the story is quite long, and remember that what I'm about to tell you is based on historical fact."

He paused to collect his thoughts and then began, "When he was a young man, Washington Irving came to stay for a while in this quiet valley, surrounded by rolling hills. He made friends with the local school teacher, Jesse Merwin, who had come from Connecticut, and they used to visit this pond to fish and swap stories. The pond is now known as Merwin's Pond.[3]

"Jesse was much interested in the local lore and it is likely that the inhabitants of Kinderhook had told him about Hendrick Hudson and his crew bowling in the Catskills, many believing that the ghosts of the explorers did indeed haunt the mountains. They would have pointed out, too, that on clear days the outline of the mountains against the sky took on the form of an old man stretched out fast asleep.".

At this point Brom was tempted to interrupt to say how much he thought the flesh and blood man by his side looked like the one made of stone, but he remained silent and let the story teller go on.

"Jesse probably learned, also, that some of the Hessian troopers who had fought in the war had decided to settle in Kinderhook[4] and that soon after they had done so, there sprang up a legend of the headless trooper who at night rose from his grave in the churchyard to ride through the countryside."[5]

Once again the boy shivered, for the headless horseman now seemed too close for comfort. The old man went on.

"The school teacher passed the tales he had heard along to his writer friend, who was likewise much interested in them. Jesse also told Irving a bit about himself. He had married Jane van Dyck,[6] the daughter of a wealthy Dutch farmer, whose farmhouse lay just to the southeast of here." The old man broke off for a moment to turn and point towards the hill beyond the dam. Then he faced back to Brom and resumed his story.

"It is thought, too, that Jesse may have told Irving that while courting Jane van Dyck he had had a rival, Abram van Alstyne, who wanted to discourage Jesse's attentions to Jane and so one night had masqueraded as the headless Hessian trooper,[7] hoping to frighten the schoolmaster so much that he would leave Kinderhook.

"We know for a fact that Irving used Jesse as a model for the Ichabod Crane of his story, since once he noted on a letter from Merwin that it came from 'the original of Ichabod Crane.'[8]

"Also, when the author came back to visit Kinderhook, he is supposed to have told one of its residents that Abram van

The Merwin Farm House, where Ichabod Crane Lived
From a photograph

Alstyne was likewise the original of Brom Bones.[9] You, Brom, are related to the model for the Brom of the story, the laughing rider at the end of your dream whose head was where it belonged."

"NOW I know why he looked so much like ME!" Brom cried out in excitement.

The old man grinned. "There is more I should tell you so you will know what I meant when I spoke about tracing parts of Irving's stories to this region."

"But I DO see already. There's the legend of Hendrick Hudson and his crew bowling, the view of the old man asleep in the mountains, the schoolmaster, and the story of the headless trooper," the boy said.

"Well, there's more," the old man replied, and went on to explain. "At the beginning of his story, Washington Irving places Sleepy Hollow near the village of Tarrytown, about a hundred miles south of here on the river. Now it is likely that he had not originally wished the story to be attached to that particular region. In fact, his general descriptions of the countryside match more closely what we have here.[10]

"With his earlier writings, Irving had unintentionally aroused bitter feelings on the part of some old Dutch families who thought he was making fun of them.[11] Being older and wiser when he wrote 'The Legend of Sleepy Hollow,' it would be natural for him to decide to take no more chances of giving offense and thus remove his story to a safe distance from its original source. There is a good reason to believe, Brom, that you and I are sitting right now in Sleepy Hollow!"

The old man fell silent, for he had come to the end. As they sat there together, Brom's head was swimming with thoughts and he had difficulty in sorting them out.

One thing he did know, though, was that he didn't mind the idea, anymore, of returning to school, since he had so much to tell his friends. In fact, he felt good to think he was a descendent of the original settlers of Kinderhook and was related to a man who had served as the model for a character in a famous American story.

Chapter 4

Return Journey

THE TIME HAD PASSED so quickly that neither man nor boy could believe the afternoon was coming to an end and that Brom should be on his way home to the farm.

As they packed up their things to leave, the old man said, "I'll show you a new way back," and whistling to Wolf, he arose.

When the three descended the hill, going west, away from the pond, Brom thought he could hear the shouting and laughter of children being let out of school. In a few moments they reached the bottom of the hill and, there on their right, Brom saw a small white building, much in need of repair.

"That's Jesse Merwin's schoolhouse," the old man said. "It isn't the original one Washington Irving saw when he first came to Kinderhook, and that's why the marker only refers to this as the site, even though Jesse taught in this building too.[12] There is talk of moving this schoolhouse which will hurt its historical importance if they do."

Brom assumed that the voices must have come from the schoolhouse, but the building was empty and obviously had not been used for a long time. There were no sounds of voices

The Site of Ichabod Crane's Schoolhouse

now, only the cawings of crows and the slurring notes of a blue jay, startled, perhaps, by the three travelers on the road. The boy supposed, then, that his imagination had been playing tricks on him and that what he had heard had been only the noises of birds.

Turning to the right, they soon came to another building, set back somewhat from the road at the end of a long cornfield bordered by trees. The house had tall red brick walls, topped by a high-peaked and low-sloping roof. As they came closer Brom could see there was some sort of sign by the road. Running up to the marker, he found that it identified the place as the Van Alen homestead, built in 1736, and that, according to tradition, Katrina van Tassel was supposed to have lived there. Brom turned in amazement to the old man, for Katrina van Tassel was the girl Ichabod Crane had fallen in love with in "The Legend of Sleepy Hollow."

Smiling at the boy's surprise, the old man said, "This house

was here, looking much as it does now, when Washington Irving first came to Kinderhook. It is perhaps the best example of early Dutch architecture to be found in our country today.[13] The famous writer used it as a model for Van Tassel's farmhouse described in his story, and that's why the marker says what it does. But it's getting late and we must move along."

As they walked away from the house, Brom thought he heard, once more, noises of shouting and laughter. This time it sounded as though there was a great party going on, like the one Ichabod Crane had been to when frightened by the headless horseman.

When Brom looked back, though, the house stood deserted and silent. The boy glanced at the old man, thinking he might be able to explain the sounds. Brom felt more than ever that there was something unreal and mysterious about his companion, but the old man seemed so far away in his thoughts that Brom said nothing.

Turning south, they retraced their steps for a bit, passing by the old schoolhouse once more. From there Irving had studied the Van Alen house while waiting from Merwin to finish the day's teaching. After walking about a mile they came to a tall two-story house, its yellow paint peeling off in places showing red brick beneath. The old man stopped and Brom wondered if this were another place Washington Irving had used as a model.

When he asked about it, the old man replied, "No, but there IS a connection here with the writer. This house belonged to the eighth President of the United States, the first of our Presidents not born under the British flag. In fact, Martin van Buren was born in Kinderhook in his father's tavern after we had become free of England's rule.

"Washington Irving was a friend of Van Buren's and visited him here at Lindenwald. Even before Van Buren owned the place, this is where Irving stayed[14] when he got ideas for the well known stories he later wrote while in England. I brought you this way on purpose, Brom, for it isn't every small American town which can boast of having a President's home

Lindenwald

From a photograph

and other such rich historical associations."

They moved on past the old yellow house, since the sun was getting low and Brom knew he should hurry or Gram would be worried about him. They were not far from the farm now and on this last lap of the journey he had been thinking constantly about the old man.

The boy was convinced that the likeness of his climbing companion in the dream to the old man of the mountains was too

Martin Van Buren

From an old daguerreotype

close to be sheer coincidence. Also, how was it that he seemed so familiar with what had happened so very long ago, almost as if he had been there himself?

Recalling the far away look in the old man's eyes when they

had talked of the bowlers, Brom felt sure his friend must have seen them. And why had the old man been so amused when Brom had asked him about Rip van Winkle?

Could it be that Rip van Winkle had actually lived and that this old man was a descendent of his? He couldn't be Rip van Winkle himself, for if he HAD lived, Rip would have died long ago — or, would he? A shadow of doubt crept into the boy's mind.

Brom had been bursting to ask about the resemblance, but had been too shy. Now, at long last, he had summoned up enough courage and was about to do so. Just at that moment he heard Gram calling his name and turned to answer. When he turned back to put the question to his friend, Brom found that both he and the dog had vanished.

As the boy stepped into the house, he could hardly overcome his disappointment. Something inside him told him that he would never see the old man again and that his question might never be answered.

When he went up to bed that night, though, he felt better, for Gram had told him something at suppertime which had set him at ease. When he had asked her if she had ever read "Rip van Winkle" or "The Legend of Sleepy Hollow," she had nodded and said, "Oh, yes, both of them. The man who wrote them lived here in Kinderhook for a while and that is a story in itself. When we have more time, I'll tell you about it."

Brom almost replied, "I've heard it already," but stopped himself, since he wasn't sure whether Gram would understand about the dream, the old man, and Wolf.

Gram went on. "Some people, you know, believe that old Rip and his dog still sleep in the mountains and that every twenty years the two awake and roam the countryside for a few days. There are those who claim to have seen them and they say the old man has some sort of magical powers. But I mustn't be putting ideas into your head."

Brom was glad now that he'd said nothing. This, then, was the answer. It also explained why his dream had been just like the stories, and why he'd heard voices and laughter from the empty buildings when homeward bound, for the old man had clearly wanted it that way.

Brom never forgot his magical friend who had gone back to sleep in the mountains. He thought of him often, when on later visits to the farm, he would look out his window and see the Catskills outlined against the evening sky.

A Biography

Washington Irving

W ASHINGTON IRVING, son of a Scottish middle-
class merchant, was born in New York on April 3,
1783. As the last and eleventh child of William and
Sarah Irving, he was named after the man who was to become
first President of the United States. In his middle twenties he
formed a deep attachment to Matilda Hoffman and, expecting
to marry her, was plunged into grief when she died in 1809.

It was then that he first visited Kinderhook, seeking comfort in the quiet and peace of the countryside. For two months
he stayed with his friends, the van Nesses, whose home was
later to become the home of President Martin van Buren and
which, as such, Irving was to revisit in 1855.

While in Kinderhook, Irving came to know Jesse Merwin,
and they remained friends for the rest of their lives. The
schoolteacher had such high regard for the writer that he named
one of his sons after him. That Jesse Merwin was the original
of Ichabod Crane was testified to by Martin van Buren, who
signed a certificate to that effect in 1846, while Irving made
a note of the same fact five years later on a letter he had received from Merwin. In answer to that letter, Irving wrote to
Merwin recalling with pleasure his early associations with the

for himself, the old man and Wolf. All the while they were eating, Brom kept glancing at the old man. He was fascinated with his resemblance to the man of the mountains, but said nothing, though he felt there was something mysterious about it.

As they were finishing the last crumbs of cake, Brom heard a rumbling noise to the west and jumped up in alarm.

"Is that a thunderstorm coming up, do you think?"

"Could be; or it might be Hendrick Hudson and his crew at their bowling in the Catskills," the old man replied with a smile.

Just then there were several more thunderous peals and they did indeed sound like balls rolling along a great alley, then crashing against bowling pins at the end.

"What do you mean?" Brom asked.

"Don't you know about Hendrick Hudson?" The old man replied with surprise.

"Sure," Brom answered, "we learned about him in school. The Hudson River was named after him. But what did you mean about him and his crew bowling in the mountains?"

"Well, there is a legend that ever since Hudson first sailed up our river in his ship, the Half Moon, over three hundred and fifty years ago, he has returned with his crew every twenty years to inspect the scenes of their explorations. At such times they go up into the mountains where there is a hollow with a leveled off place and it is there that they bowl. When a thunderstorm brews behind the Catskills people say that it is the Dutchmen come back to their game."

"You DON'T really believe that, do you?" Brom asked.

The old man did not answer, but instead continued to smile with a far away look in his eyes, as if he were living in long ago times. "I'll tell you something which IS known for a fact," he said. "In 1609 Hendrick Hudson anchored at a bend, or corner, of the river only a few miles from here. When he came ashore the Indians were friendly to him and their children gathered on the riverbank to see the strange ship which had come to their land. So it is that this town, where we now are, schoolteacher: talks with his friend in which were passed on anecdotes of local characters, a fishing expedition to the lake in company with Congressman van Alen, recollections of the schoolhouse mixed with regret that the old building had to be replaced by a new one.

During this period at Kinderhook, Irving finished the satirical and humorous work, his *Knickerbocker History of New York,* which outraged certain Dutch families because of the direct use of their names, but which also established his reputation as a writer. He first heard of this outrage during a visit to Albany, New York, and then later in England[15] while working on *The Sketch Book,* the collection of stories containing "Rip van Winkle" and "The Legend of Sleepy Hollow," the latter written in London during 1819. Because of the bitterness he had unintentionally fostered, he undoubtedly resolved to be more careful in the future. *The Sketch Book* was an immediate success, serving to strengthen his reputation as an author both at home and abroad.

In his notes made when traveling, and upon which he was to base much of his writing, Irving makes frequent reference to the effect which the surrounding scenery had upon him. Among the earliest of these are records of a trip up the Hudson River in 1800 in which he speaks of being bewitched by the distant Catskills, though, by his own admission, it was not until after "Rip van Winkle" had been written that he was actually to visit these mountains.[16]

For seventeen years, from 1815 to 1832, Washington Irving spent his time abroad, traveling and writing. Upon return to America in 1832, he visited Tarrytown for the first documented time and purchased Sunnyside, the home he established for himself at Tarrytown, many years after writing "The Legend of Sleepy Hollow." He made an adventuresome trip to the American west and wrote about it.

During the four years 1842-1846, he served his country as Minister to Spain. He retired to Sunnyside after 1846 and on November 28, 1859, in his seventy-sixth year, Washington Irving died, shortly after finishing his last work, *The Life of*

George Washington, a five volume biography of his boyhood hero. Thus came to an end the life of a man who was to have a profound influence on early American writing, recognized both at home and abroad as the first American man of letters, the father of American Literature.

Footnotes and Bibliography

[1] Half Moon in Kinderhook. *A History of Old Kinderhook,* pp. 1-8, by Edward A. Collier, ©1914, published by G.P. Putnam's Sons, The Knickerbocker Press.

[2] Hessians with Burgoyne. *A History of Old Kinderhook,* pp. 188-189.

[3] Washington Irving with Jesse Merwin in Kinderhook. *A History of Old Kinderhook,* pp. 24, 362. Also, *The Life and Letters of Washington Irving,* p. 80, Vol. IV, by his nephew Pierre M. Irving, published by G.P. Putnam, New York, 1867.

[4] Hessians settle in Kinderhook. *A History of Old Kinderhook, pp. 188-189.*

[5] Rubezahl legends of German source where Hesse is located. "Both the incident of the chase and that of the hurling of the 'head' may be found in the Rubezahl legends." *The Life of Washington Irving,* p. 183, Vol. I, by Stanley T. Williams, professor of English at Yale, published by N.Y. Oxford University Press, 1935.

[6] J. Merwin & J. van Dyck. 1809 and 1810 tax lists will show value of Peter C. van Dyck's farm and his children including Jane, born 1786, who married Jesse Merwin from Connecticut, born 1784, on 16 Oct. 1808, and in 1810, having lived with her father, Peter C. van Dyck, they took over her father's farm upon his death. Louise Hardenbrook, Columbia County (NY) Historical Society Librarian, did research that shows this.

[7] Abram (Brom) van Alstyne as the headless Hessian trooper. Letter to the editor of *The New York Times Saturday Review,* 19 March 1898, from Harold van Santvoord, author of "Half Holidays." "An aged lady of tenacious powers of memory...gave...a lively account of the exploits of the redoubtable Brom Bones—one Abram van Alstyne, as Irving himself confessed." Also, *The Life of Washington Irving,* p. 429, Vol. I, by Stanley T. Williams. "Brom Bones was also identified with Brom van Alstyne, a character in the village of Kinderhook..."

[8] Jesse Merwin original Ichabod Crane. *The Life and Letters of Washington Irving,* p. 80, Vol. IV, by P.M. Irving.

[9] See footnote 7.

[10] Irving's 1809 descriptions of Kinderhook match those in *The Legend of Sleepy Hollow. The Life and Letters of Washington Irving,* p. 229, Vol. I, by P.M. Irving.

[11] Bitter feelings of some Dutch families. *The Life and Letters of Washington Irving,* pp. 242, 246, Vol. I, by P.M. Irving.

[12] Merwin's schoolhouse. *The Life and Letters of Washington Irving,* p. 80, Vol. I, by P.M. Irving. Also, *A History of Old Kinderhook,* p. 362.

[13] Van Alen homestead best example of early Dutch architecture. Richard H. Howland, president, National Trust for Historic Preservation, 24 August 1959 letter states, "Thank you for consulting us about the van Alen House in Kinderhook, N.Y. There seems to be little doubt of its qualification as the outstanding surviving example of true Dutch architecture in America."

[14] Washington Irving visits Martin van Buren at Lindenwald. *A History of Old Kinderhook,* p. 232, "In September (1855), Washington Irving visits ex-President van Buren at Lindenwald, where more than fifty years before he had been tutor in the family of Judge William P. van Ness and commenced his literary career."

[15] Outrage of Dutch families. *The Life and Letters of Washington Irving,* pp 242, 246, Vol. I, by P.M. Irving.

[16] After writing *Rip Van Winkle,* visits Catskills. *The Life and Letters of Washington Irving,* p. 53, Vol. III, by P.M. Irving. Irving said, "When I wrote the story, I had never been on the Catskills." In 1833 Irving visited for the first time Kingston and other old Dutch villages on the skirts of the Catskill Mountains.

THE LEGEND OF
SLEEPY HOLLOW

(FOUND AMONG THE PAPERS
OF THE LATE DIEDRICH KNICKERBOCKER.)

A pleasing land of drowsy head it was,
Of dreams that wave before the half-shut eye;
And of gay castles in the clouds that pass,
Forever flushing round a summer sky.
Castle of Indolence.

IN THE BOSOM of one of those spacious coves which indent the eastern shore of the Hudson, at that broad expansion of the river denominated by the ancient Dutch navigators the Tappan Zee, and where they always prudently shortened sail, and implored the protection of St. Nicholas when they crossed, there lies a small market town or rural port, which by some is called Greensburgh, but which is more generally and properly known by the name of Tarry Town. This name was given it, we are told, in former days, by the good housewives of the adjacent country, from the inveterate propensity of their husbands to linger about the village tavern on market days. Be that as it may, I do not vouch for the fact, but merely advert to it, for the sake of being precise and authentic. Not far from this village, perhaps about three miles, there is a little valley or rather lap of land among high hills, which is one of the quietest places in the whole world. A small brook glides through it, with just murmur enough to lull one to repose; and the occasional whistle of a quail, or tapping of a woodpecker, is almost the only sound that ever breaks in upon the uniform tranquillity.

I recollect that, when a stripling, my first exploit in squirrel-shooting was in a grove of tall walnut-trees that shades one side of the valley. I had wandered into it at noon-time, when all nature is peculiarly quiet, and was startled by the roar of my own gun, as it broke the sabbath stillness around, and was prolonged and reverberated by the angry echoes. If ever I should wish for a retreat whither I might steal from the world and its distractions, and dream quietly away the remnant of a troubled life, I know of none more promising than this little valley.

From the listless repose of the place, and the peculiar character of its inhabitants, who are descendants from the original Dutch settlers, this sequestered glen has long been known by the name of SLEEPY HOLLOW, and its rustic lads are called the Sleepy Hollow Boys throughout all the neighboring country. A drowsy, dreamy influence seems to hang over the land, and to pervade the very atmosphere. Some say that the place was bewitched by a high German doctor, during the early days of the settlement; others, that an old Indian chief, the prophet or wizard of his tribe, held his powwows there before the country was discovered by Master Hendrick Hudson. Certain it is the place still continues under the sway of some witching power, that holds a spell over the minds of the good people, causing them to walk in a continual reverie. They are given to all kinds of marvellous beliefs; are subject to trances and visions, and frequently see strange sights, and hear music and voices in the air. The whole neighborhood abounds with local tales, haunted spots, and twilight superstitions; stars shoot and meteors glare oftener across the valley than in any other part of the country, and the nightmare, with her whole nine fold, seems to make it the favorite scene of her gambols.

The dominant spirit, however, that haunts this enchanted region, and seems to be commander-in-chief of all the powers of the air, is the apparition of a figure on horseback without a head. It is said by some to be the ghost of a Hessian trooper whose head had been carried away by a cannon-ball, in some nameless battle during the revolutionary war, and who is ever and anon seen by the country folk, hurring along in the gloom of night, as if on the wind. His haunts are not confined to the valley, but extend at times to the adjacent roads, and especially to the vicinity of a church that is at no great distance. Indeed, certain of the most authentic historians of those parts, who have been careful in collecting and collating the floating facts concerning this spectre, allege, that the body of the trooper having been in the churchyard, the ghost rides forth to the scene of the battle in nightly quest of his head, and that the rushing speed with which he sometimes passes along the hollow, like a midnight blast, is owing to his being belated, and in a hurry to get back to the churchyard before day-break.

Such is the general purport of this legendary superstition, which has furnished materials for many a wild story in that region of shadows; and the spectre is known at all the country firesides, by the name of the Headless Horseman of Sleepy Hollow.

It is remarkable, that the visionary propensity I have mentioned is not confined to the native inhabitants of the valley, but is unconsciously imbibed by everyone who resides there for a time. However wide awake they may have been before they entered that sleepy region, they are sure, in a little time, to inhale the witching influence of the air and begin to grow imaginative — to dream dreams, and see apparitions.

I mention this peaceful spot with all possible laud; for it is in such little retired Dutch valleys, found here and there embosomed in the great State of New York, that population, manners, and customs remain fixed, while the great torrent of migration and improvement, which is making such incessant changes in other parts of this restless country, sweeps by them unobserved. They are like those little nooks of still water, which border a rapid stream, where we may see the straw and bubble riding quietly at anchor, or slowly revolving in their mimic harbor, undisturbed by the rush of the passing current. Though many years have elapsed since I trod the drowsy shades of

Sleepy Hollow, yet I question whether I should not find the same trees and the same families vegetating in its sheltered bosom.

In this by-place of nature there abode, in a remote period of American history, that is to say, some thirty years since, a worthy wight by the name of Ichabod Crane, who sojourned, or, as he expressed it, "tarried," in Sleepy Hollow, for the purpose of instructing the children of the vicinity. He was a native of Connecticut, a State which supplies the Union with pioneers for the mind as well as for the forest, and sends forth yearly its legions of frontier woodmen and country schoolmasters. The cognomen of Crane was not inapplicable to his person. He was tall, but exceedingly lank, with narrow shoulders, long arms and legs, hands that dangled a mile out of his sleeves, feet that might have served for shovels, and his whole frame most loosely hung together. His head was small, and flat at top, with huge ears, large green glassy eyes, and a long snipe nose, so that it looked like a weathercock perched upon his spindle neck, to tell which way the wind blew. To see him striding along the profile of a hill on a windy day, with his clothes bagging and fluttering about him, one might have mistaken him for the genius of famine descending upon the earth, or some scarecrow eloped from a cornfield.

His school-house was a low building of one large room, rudely constructed of logs; the windows partly glazed, and partly patched with leafs of copy-books. It was most ingeniously secured at vacant hours, by a withe twisted in the handle of the door, and stakes set against the window-shutters; so that though a thief might get in with perfect ease he would find some embarrassment in getting out; — an idea most probably borrowed by the architect, Yost Van Houten, from the mystery of an eelpot. The school-house stood in a rather lonely but pleasant situation, just at the foot of a woody hill, with a brook running close by, and a formidable birch-tree growing at one end of it. From hence the low murmur of his pupils' voices, conning over their lessons, might be heard of a drowsy summer's day, like the hum of a beehive; interrupted now and then by the authoritative voice of the master, in the tone of menace or command; or, peradventure, by the appalling sound of the birch, as he urged some tardy loiterer along the flowery path of knowledge. Truth to say, he was a conscientious man, that ever bore in mind the golden maxim, "spare the rod and spoil the child." Ichabod Crane's scholars certainly were not spoiled.

I would not have it imagined, however, that he was one of those cruel potentates of the school, who joy in the smart of their subjects; on the contrary, he administered justice with discrimination rather than severity; taking the burden off the backs of the weak, and laying it on those of the strong. Your mere puny stripling, that winced at the least flourish of the rod, was passed by with indulgence; but the claims of justice were satisfied by inflicting a double portion on some little, tough, wrong-headed, broad-skirted Dutch urchin, who sulked and swelled and grew dogged and sullen beneath the birch. All this he called "doing his duty by their parents;" and he never inflicted a chastisement without following it by the assurance so consolatory to the smarting urchin, that "he would remember it and thank him for it the longest day he had to live."

When school hours were over, he was even the companion and playmate of the larger boys; and on holiday afternoons would convey some of the smaller ones home, who happened to have pretty sisters or good housewives for mothers, noted for the comforts of the cupboard. Indeed, it behooved him to keep on good terms with his pupils. The revenue arising from his school was small, and would have been scarcely sufficient to furnish him with daily bread, for he was a huge feeder, and though lank, had the dilating powers of an anaconda; but to help out his maintenance, he was, according to country custom in those parts, boarded and lodged at the houses of the farmers, whose children he instructed. With these he lived successively a week at a time, thus going the rounds of the neighborhood, with all his worldly effects tied up in a cotton handkerchief.

That all this might not be too onerous on the purses of his

rustic patrons, who are apt to consider the costs of schooling a grievous burden, and schoolmasters as mere drones, he had various ways of rendering himself both useful and agreeable. He assisted the farmers occasionally in the lighter labors of their farms; helped to make hay; mended the fences; took the horses to water; drove the cows from pasture; and cut wood for the winter fire. He laid aside, too, all the dominant dignity and absolute sway with which he lorded it in his little empire, the school, and became wonderfully gentle and ingratiating. He found favor in eyes of the mothers by petting the children, particularly the youngest; and like the lion bold, which whilom so magnanimously the lamb did hold, he would sit with a child on one knee, and rock a cradle with his foot for whole hours together.

In addition to his other vocations, he was the singing-master of the neighborhood, and picked up many bright shillings by instructing the young folks in psalmody. It was a matter of no little vanity to him on Sundays, to take his station in front of the church gallery, with a band of chosen singers; where, in his own mind, he completely carried away the palm from the parson. Certain it is, his voice resounded far above all the rest of the congregation, and there are peculiar quavers still to be heard in that church, and which may even be heard half a mile off, quite to the opposite side of the mill-pond, on a still Sunday morning, which are said to be legitimately descended from the nose of Ichabod Crane. Thus, by divers little makeshifts, in that ingenious way which is commonly denominated "by hook and by crook," the worthy pedagogue got on tolerably enough, and was thought, by all who understood nothing of the labor of head-work, to have a wonderful easy life of it.

The schoolmaster is generally a man of some importance in the female circle of a rural neighborhood; being considered a kind of idle gentleman-like personage, of vastly superior taste and accomplishments to the rough country swains, and, indeed, inferior in learning only to the parson. His appearance, therefore, is apt to occasion some little stir at the tea-table of a farm-house, and the addition of a supernumerary dish of

cakes or sweetmeats, or peradventure, the parade of a silver
tea-pot. Our man of letters, therefore, was peculiarly happy
in the smiles of all the country damsels. How he would figure
among them in the churchyard, between services on Sundays!
gather grapes for them from the wild vines that overrun the
surrounding trees; reciting for their amusement all the epitaphs
on the tombstones; or sauntering with a whole bevy of them
along the banks of the adjacent mill-pond; while the more
bashful country bumpkins hung sheepishly back, envying his
superior elegance and address.

From his half itinerant life, also, he was a kind of travell-
ing gazette, carrying the whole budget of local gossip from
house to house; so that his appearance was always greeted with
satisfaction. He was, moreover, esteemed by the women as a
man of great erudition, for he had read several books quite
through, and was a perfect master of Cotton Mather's History
of New England Witchcraft, in which, by the way, he most
firmly and potently believed.

He was, in fact, an odd mixture of small shrewdness and
simple credulity. His appetite for the marvellous and his powers
of digesting it were equally extraordinary; and both had been
increased by his residence in this spell-bound region. No tale
was too gross or monstrous for his capacious swallow. It was
often his delight, after his school was dismissed in the afternoon, to stretch himself on the rich bed of clover, bordering
the little brook that whimpered by his school-house, and there
con over old Mather's direful tales, until the gathering dusk
of evening made the printed page a mere mist before his eyes.
Then, as he wended his way, by swamp and stream and awful
woodland, to the farm-house where he happened to be quar-
tered, every sound of nature, at that witching hour, fluttered
his excited imagination: the moan of the whip-poor-will* from
the hillside; the boding cry of the tree-toad, that harbinger of
storm; the dreary hooting of the screech-owl; or the sudden

---

*The whip-poor-will is a bird which is only heard at night. It receives its
name from its note, which is thought to resemble those words.

rustling in the thicket of birds frightened from their roost. The fire-flies, too, which sparkled most vividly in the darkest places, now and then startled him, as one of uncommon brightness would stream across his path; and if, by chance, a huge blockhead of a beetle came winging his blundering flight against him, the poor varlet was ready to give up the ghost, with the idea that he was struck with a witch's token. His only resource on such occasions, either to drown thought, or drive away evil spirits, was to sing psalm tunes; — and the good people of Sleepy Hollow, as they sat by their doors of an evening, were often filled with awe, at hearing his nasal melody, "in linked sweetness long drawn out," floating from the distant hill, or along the dusky road.

Another of his sources of fearful pleasure was, to pass long winter evenings with the old Dutch wives as they sat spinning by the fire, with a row of apples roasting and sputtering along the hearth, and listen to their marvellous tales of ghosts, and goblins, and haunted fields and haunted brooks, and haunted bridges and haunted houses, and particularly of the headless horseman, or galloping Hessian of the Hollow, as they sometimes called him. He would delight them equally by his anecdotes of witchcraft, and of the direful omens and portentous sights and sounds in the air, which prevailed in the early times of Connecticut; and would frighten them wofully with speculations upon comets and shooting stars, and with the alarming fact that the world did absolutely turn around, and that they were half the time topsy-turvy!

But if there was a pleasure in all this, while snugly cuddling in the chimney corner of a chamber that was all of a ruddy glow from the crackling wood fire, and where, of course, no spectre dared to show its face, it was dearly purchased by the terrors of his subsequent walk homewards. What fearful shapes and shadows beset his path, amidst the dim and ghastly glare of a snowy night! — With what wistful look did he eye every trembling ray of light streaming across the the waste fields from some distant window! — How often was he appalled by some shrub covered with snow, which like a sheeted spectre beset his very path! — How often did he shrink with curdling awe at the sound of his own steps on the frosty crust beneath his feet; and dread to look over his shoulder, lest he should behold some uncouth being tramping close behind him! — and how often was he thrown into complete dismay by some rushing blast, howling among the trees, in the idea that it was the galloping Hessian on one of his nightly scourings!

All these, however, were mere terrors of the night, phantoms of the mind, that walk in darkness: and though he had seen many spectres in his time, and been more than once beset by Satan in divers shapes, in his lonely perambulations, yet daylight put an end to all these evils; and he would have passed a pleasant life of it, in despite of the Devil and all his works, if his path had not been crossed by a being that causes more perplexity to mortal man than ghosts, goblins, and the whole race of witches put together; and that was — a woman.

Among the musical disciples who assembled, one evening in each week, to receive his instructions in psalmody, was Katrina Van Tassel, the daughter and only child of a substantial Dutch farmer. She was a blooming lass of fresh eighteen; plump as a partridge; ripe and melting and rosy-cheeked as one of her father's peaches, and universally famed, not merely for her beauty, but her vast expectations. She was withal a little of a coquette, as might be perceived even in her dress, which was a mixture of ancient and modern fashions, as most suited to set off her charms. She wore the ornaments of pure yellow gold, which her great-great-grandmother had brought over from Saardam; the tempting stomacher of the olden time, and withal a provokingly short petticoat, to display the prettiest foot and ankle in the country round.

Ichabod Crane had a soft and foolish heart towards the sex; and it is not to be wondered at, that so tempting a morsel soon found favor in his eyes, more especially after he had visited her in her paternal mansion. Old Baltus Van Tassel was a perfect picture of a thriving, contented, liberal-hearted farmer. He seldom, it is true, sent either his eyes or his thoughts beyond the boundaries of his own farm; but within these, everything was snug, happy and well-conditioned. He was satisfied with his wealth, but not proud of it; and piqued himself upon the hearty abundance, rather than the style in which he lived. His stronghold was situated on the banks of the Hudson, in one of those green, sheltered, fertile nooks, in which the Dutch farmers are so fond of nestling. A great elm-tree spread its broad branches over it; at the foot of which bubbled up a spring of the softest and sweetest water, in a little well, formed of a barrel; and then stole sparkling away through the grass, to a neighboring brook, that babbled along among alders and dwarf willows. Hard by the farm-house was a vast barn, that might have served for a church; every window and crevice of which seemed bursting forth with the treasures of the farm; the flail was busily resounding within it from morning to night; swallows and martins skimmed twittering about the eaves; and rows of pigeons, some with one eye turned up, as if watching the weather, some with their heads under their wings, or buried in their bosoms, and others, swelling, and cooing, and bowing about their dames, were enjoying the sunshine on the roof. Sleek unwieldy porkers were grunting in the repose and abundance of their pens, from whence sallied forth, now and then, troops of sucking pigs, as if to sniff the air. A stately squadron of snowy geese were riding in an adjoining pond, convoying whole fleets of ducks; regiments of turkeys were gobbling through the farm-yard, and guinea-fowls fretting about it like ill-tempered housewives, with their peevish, discontented cry. Before the barn door strutted the gallant cock, that pattern of a husband, a warrior, and a fine gentleman; clapping his burnished wings and crowing in the pride and gladness of his heart — sometimes tearing up the earth with his feet, and then generously calling his ever-hungry family of wives and children to enjoy the rich morsel which he had discovered.

The pedagogue's mouth watered, as he looked upon this sumptuous promise of luxurious winter fare. In his devouring mind's eye, he pictured to himself every roasting pig running about, with a pudding in its belly, and an apple in its mouth; the pigeons were snugly put to bed in a comfortable pie, and tucked in with a coverlet of crust; the geese were swimming in their own gravy; and the ducks pairing cosily in dishes, like snug married couples, with a decent competency of onion sauce. In the porkers he saw carved out the future sleek side of bacon, and juicy relishing ham; not a turkey, but he beheld daintily trussed up, with its gizzard under its wing, and, peradventure, a necklace of savory sausages; and even bright chanticleer himself lay sprawling on his back, in a side dish, with uplifted claws, as if craving that quarter which his chivalrous spirit disdained to ask while living.

As the enraptured Ichabod fancied all this, and as he rolled his great green eyes over the fat meadow lands, the rich fields of wheat, of rye, of buckwheat, and Indian corn, and the orchards burdened with ruddy fruit, which surrounded the warm tenement of Van Tassel, his heart yearned after the damsel who was to inherit these domains, and his imagination expanded with the idea, how they might be readily turned into cash, and the money invested in immense tracts of wild land, and shingle palaces in the wilderness. Nay, his busy fancy already realized his hopes, and presented to him the blooming Katrina, with a whole family of children mounted on the top of a wagon loaded with household trumpery, with pots and kettles dangling beneath; and he beheld himself bestriding a pacing mare, with a colt at her heels, setting out for Kentucky, Tennessee — or the Lord knows where!

When he entered the house, the conquest of his heart was complete. It was one of those spacious farm-houses, with high-ridged, but lowly-sloping roofs, built in the style handed down from the first Dutch settlers. The low projecting eaves forming a piazza along the front, capable of being closed up in bad weather. Under this were hung flails, harness, various utensils of husbandry, and nets for fishing in the neighboring river. Benches were built along the sides for summer use; and a great spinning-wheel at one end, and a churn at the other, showed the various uses to which this important porch might be devoted. From this piazza the wonderful Ichabod entered the hall, which formed the centre of the mansion, and the place

of usual residence. Here, rows of resplendent pewter, ranged
on a long dresser, dazzled his eyes. In one corner stood a huge
bag of wool, ready to be spun; in another, a quantity of linsey-
woolsey just from the loom; ears of Indian corn, and strings
of dried apples and peaches, hung in gay festoons along the
walls, mingled with the gaud of red peppers; and a door left
ajar, gave him a peep into the best parlor, where the claw-
footed chairs, and dark mahogany tables, shone like mirrors;
andirons, with their accompanying shovel and tongs, glistened
from their covert of asparagus tops; mock-oranges and conch
shells decorated the mantlepiece; strings of various colored
birds' eggs were suspended above it; a great ostrich egg was
hung from the centre of the room, and a corner cupboard,
knowingly left open, displayed immense treasures of old silver
and well-mended china.

From the moment Ichabod laid his eyes upon these regions
of delight, the peace of his mind was at an end, and his only
study was how to gain the affections of the peerless daughter
of Van Tassel. In this enterprise, however, he had more real
difficulties than generally fell to the lot of a knight-errant of
yore, who seldom had anything but giants, enchanters, fiery
dragons, and such like easily conquered adversaries, to contend with, and had to make his way merely through gates of
iron and brass, and walls of adamant to the castle-keep, where
the lady of his heart was confined; all which he achieved as
easily as a man would carve his way to the centre of a Christmas
pie, and then the lady gave him her hand as a matter of course.
Ichabod, on the contrary, had to win his way to the heart of
a country coquette, beset with a labyrinth of whims and
caprices, which were forever presenting new difficulties and
impediments, and he had to encounter a host of fearful adversaries of real flesh and blood, and numerous rustic admirers,
who beset every portal to her heart; keeping a watchful and
angry eye upon each other, but ready to fly out in the common cause against any new competitor.

Among these, the most formidable was a burly, roaring,
roystering blade, of the name of Abraham, or according to

the Dutch abbreviation, Brom Van Brunt, the hero of the country round, which rung with his feats of strength and hardihood. He was broad-shouldered and double-jointed, with short, curly black hair, and a bluff, but not unpleasant countenance, having a mingled air of fun and arrogance. From his Herculean frame and great powers of limb, he had received the nickname of BROM BONES, by which he was universally known. He was famed for great knowledge and skill in horsemanship, being as dexterous on horseback as a Tartar. He was foremost at all races and cock-fights, and with the ascendancy which bodily strength always acquires in rustic life, was the umpire in all disputes, setting his hat on one side, and giving his decisions with an air and tone that admitted of no gainsay or appeal. He was always ready for either a fight or a frolic; had more mischief than ill-will in his composition; and with all his overbearing roughness, there was a strong dash of waggish good-humor at bottom. He had three or four boon companions of his own stamp, who regarded him as their model, and at the head of whom he scoured the country, attending every scene of feud or merriment for miles around. In cold weather, he was distinguished by a fur cap, surmounted with a flaunting fox's tail; and when the folks at a country gathering descried this well-known crest at a distance, whisking about among a squad of hard riders, they always stood by for a squall. Sometimes his crew would be heard dashing along past the farm-houses at midnight, with whoop and halloo, like a troop of Don Cossacks, and the old dames, startled out of their sleep, would listen for a moment till the hurry-scurry had clattered by, and then exclaim, "Ay, there goes Brom Bones and his gang!" The neighbors looked upon him with a mixture of awe, admiration, and good-will; and when any madcap prank or rustic brawl occurred in the vicinity, always shook their heads, and warranted Brom Bones was at the bottom of it.

This rantipole hero had for some time singled out the blooming Katrina for the object of his uncouth gallantries, and though his amorous toyings were something like the gentle caresses and endearments of a bear, yet it was whispered that she did not altogether discourage his hopes. Certain it is, his advances were signals for rival candidates to retire, who felt no inclination to cross a lion in his amours; insomuch, that when his horse was seen tied to Van Tassel's palings, on a Sunday night, a sure sign that his master was courting, or, as it is termed, "sparking" within, all other suitors passed by in despair, and carried the war into other quarters.

Such was the formidable rival with whom Ichabod Crane had to contend, and considering all things, a stouter man than he would have shrunk from the competition, and a wiser man would have despaired. He had, however, a happy mixture of pliability and perseverance in his nature; he was in form and spirit like a supple-jack — yielding, but tough; though he bent, he never broke; and though he bowed beneath the slightest pressure, yet, the moment it was away — jerk! — he was as erect, and carried his head as high as ever.

To have taken the field openly against his rival would have been madness; for he was not a man to be thwarted in his amours, any more than that stormy lover, Achilles. Ichabod, therefore, made his advances in a quiet and gently-insinuating manner. Under cover of his character of singing-master, he made frequent visits at the farm-house; not that he had anything to apprehend from the meddlesome interference of parents, which is so often a stumbling-block in the path of lovers. Balt Van Tassel was an easy indulgent soul; he loved his daughter better even than his pipe, and like a reasonable man, and an excellent father, let her have her way in everything. His notable little wife, too, had enough to do to attend to her housekeeping and manage the poultry; for, as she sagely observed, ducks and geese are foolish things, and must be looked after, but girls can take care of themselves. Thus, while the busy dame bustled about the house, or plied her spinning-wheel at one end of the piazza, honest Balt would sit smoking his evening pipe at the other, watching the achievements of a little wooden warrior, who, armed with a sword in each hand, was most valiantly fighting the wind on the pinnacle of the barn. In the meantime, Ichabod would carry on his suit with

the daughter by the side of the spring under the great elm, or
sauntering along in the twilight, that hour so favorable to the
lover's eloquence.

I profess not to know how women's hearts are wooed and
won. To me they have always been matters of riddle and admiration. Some seem to have but one vulnerable point, or door
of access; while others have a thousand avenues, and may be
captured in a thousand different ways. It is a great triumph
of skill to gain the former, but a still greater proof of
generalship to maintain possession of the latter, for a man must
battle for his fortress at every door and window. He that wins
a thousand common hearts, is therefore entitled to some
renown; but he who keeps undisputed sway over the heart of
a coquette, is indeed a hero. Certain it is, this was not the case
with the redoubtable Brom Bones; and from the moment
Ichabod Crane made his advances, the interests of the former
evidently declined: his horse was no longer seen tied at the palings on Sunday nights, and a deadly feud gradually arose between him and the preceptor of Sleepy Hollow.

Brom, who had a degree of rough chivalry in his nature,
would fain have carried matters to open warfare, and settled
their pretensions to the lady, according to the mode of those
most concise and simple reasoners, the knights-errant of
yore — by single combat; but Ichabod was too conscious of the
superior might of his adversary to enter the lists against him;
he had overheard the boast of Bones that he would "double
the schoolmaster up, and put him on a shelf," and he was too
wary to give him an opportunity. There was something ex-
tremely provoking in this obstinately pacific system; it left
Brom no alternative but to draw upon the funds of rustic wag-
gery in his disposition, and to play off boorish practical jokes
upon his rival. Ichabod became the object of whimsical
persecutions to Bones and his gang of rough riders. They har-
ried his hitherto peaceful domains; smoked out his singing-
school by stopping up the chimney; broke into the school-house
at night, in spite of its formidable fastenings of withe and
windowstakes, and turned everything topsy-turvy; so that the

poor schoolmaster began to think all the witches in the country held their meetings there. But what was still more annoy-
ing, Brom took all opportunities of turning him into ridicule
in presence of his mistress, and had a scoundrel dog whom
he taught to whine in the most ludicrous manner, and intro-
duced as a rival of Ichabod's, to instruct her in psalmody.

In this way, matters went on for some time, without pro-
ducing any material effect on the relative situations of the con-
tending powers. On a fine autumnal afternoon, Ichabod, in
pensive mood, sat enthroned on the lofty stool from whence
he usually watched all the concerns of his literary realm. In
his hand he swayed a ferule, that sceptre of despotic power;
the birch of justice reposed on three nails, behind the throne,
a constant terror to evil doers; while on the desk before him
might be seen sundry contraband articles and prohibited
weapons, detected upon the persons of idle urchins; such as
half-munched apples, popguns, whirligigs, fly-cages, and whole
legions of rampant little paper game-cocks. Apparently there
had been some appalling act of justice recently inflicted, for
the scholars were all busily intent upon their books, or slyly
whispering behind them with one eye kept upon the master;
and a kink of buzzing stillness reigned throughout the
schoolroom. It was suddenly interrupted by the appearance
of a negro in tow-cloth jacket and trowsers, a round crowned
fragment of a hat, like the cap of Mercury, and mounted on
the back of a ragged, wild, half-broken colt, which he managed
with a rope by way of halter. He came clattering up to the
school-door with an invitation to Ichabod to attend a merry-
making, or "quilting-frolic," to be held that evening at Mynheer
Van Tassel's; and having delivered his message with that air
of importance, and effort at fine language, which a negro is
apt to display on petty embassies of the kind, he dashed over
the brook, and was seen scampering away up the hollow, full
of the importance and hurry of his mission.

All was now bustle and hubbub in the late quiet schoolroom.
The scholars were hurried through their lessons, without stopping at trifles; those who were nimble, skipped over half with

impunity, and those who were tardy, had a smart application now and then in the rear, to quicken their speed, or help them over a tall word. Books were flung aside, without being put away on the shelves; ink stands were overturned, benches thrown down, and the whole school was turned loose an hour before the usual time; bursting forth like a legion of young imps, yelping and racketing about the green, in joy at their early emancipation.

The gallant Ichabod now spent at least an extra half-hour at his toilet, brushing and furbishing up his best, and indeed only suit of rusty black, and arranging his looks by a bit of broken looking-glass, that hung up in the school-house. That he might make his appearance before his mistress in the true style of a cavalier, he borrowed a horse from the farmer with whom he was domiciliated, a choleric old Dutchman, of the name of Hans Van Ripper, and thus gallantly mounted, issued forth like a knight-errant in quest of adventures. But it is meet I should, in the true spirit of romantic story, give some account of the looks and equipments of my hero and his steed. The animal he bestrode was a broken-down plough-horse, that had outlived almost everything but his viciousness. He was gaunt and shagged, with a ewe neck and head like a hammer; his rusty mane and tail were tangled and knotted with burrs; one eye had lost its pupil, and was glaring and spectral, but the other had the gleam of a genuine devil in it. Still he must have had fire and mettle in his day, if we may judge from his name, which was Gunpowder. He had, in fact, been a favorite steed of his master's, the choleric Van Ripper, who was a furious rider, and had infused, very probably, some of his own spirit into the animal; for, old and broken-down as he looked, there was more of the lurking devil in him than in any young filly in the country.

Ichabod was a suitable figure for such a steed. He rode with short stirrups, which brought his knees nearly up to the pommel of the saddle: his sharp elbows stuck out like grasshoppers'; he carried his whip perpendicularly in his hand, like a sceptre, and as the horse jogged on, the motion of his arms was not unlike the flapping of a pair of wings. A small wool hat rested on the top of his nose, for so his scanty strip of forehead might be called, and the skirts of his black coat fluttered out almost to the horse's tail. Such was the appearance of Ichabod and his steed as they shambled out of the gate of Hans Van Ripper, and it was altogether such an apparition as is seldom to be met with in broad daylight.

It was, as I have said, a fine autumnal day; the sky was clear and serene, and nature wore that rich and golden livery which we always associate with the idea of abundance. The forests had put on their sober brown and yellow, while some trees of the tenderer kind had been nipped by the frosts into brilliant dyes of orange, purple, and scarlet. Streaming files of wild ducks began to make their appearance high in the air; the bark of the squirrel might be heard from the groves of beech and hickory-nuts, and the pensive whistle of the quail at intervals from the neighboring stubble field.

The small birds were taking their farewell banquets. In the fullness of their revelry, they fluttered, chirping and frolicking, from bush to bush, and tree to tree, capricious from the very profusion and variety around them. There was the honest cockrobin, the favorite game of stripling sportsmen, with its loud querulous note, and the twittering blackbirds flying in sable clouds; and the golden-winged woodpecker, with his crimson crest, his broad black gorget, and splendid plumage; and the cedar-bird, with its red-tipt wings and yellow-tipt tail and its little monteiro cap of feathers; and the blue jay, that noisy coxcomb, in his gay light blue coat and white underclothes, screaming and chattering, nodding, and bobbing, and bowing, and pretending to be on good terms with every songster of the grove.

As Ichabod jogged slowly on his way, his eye, ever open to every symptom of culinary abundance, ranged with delight over the treasures of jolly autumn. On all sides he beheld vast stores of apples, some hanging in oppressive opulence on the trees; some gathered into baskets and barrels for the market; others heaped up in rich piles for the cider-press. Farther on

he beheld great fields of Indian corn, with its golden ears peep-
ing from their leafy coverts, and holding out the promise of
cakes and hasty-pudding; and the yellow pumpkins lying
beneath them, turning up their fair round bellies to the sun,
and giving ample prospects of the most luxurious of pies; and
anon he passed the fragrant buckwheat fields breathing the
odor of the beehive; and as he beheld them, soft anticipations
stole over his mind of dainty slap-jacks, well-buttered, and
garnished with honey or treacle, by the delicate little dimpled
hand of Katrina Van Tassel.

Thus feeding his mind with many sweet thoughts and
"sugared suppositions," he journeyed along the sides of a range
of hills which look out upon some of the goodliest scenes of
the mighty Hudson. The sun gradually wheeled his broad disk
down in the west. The wide bosom of the Tappan Zee lay
motionless and glassy, excepting that here and there a gentle
undulation waved and prolonged the blue shadow of the distant mountain. A few amber clouds floated in the sky, without
a breath of air to move them. The horizon was of a fine golden
tint, changing gradually into a pure apple green, and from that
into the deep blue of the mid-heaven. A slanting ray lingered
on the woody crests of the precipices that overhung some parts
of the river, giving greater depth to the dark gray and purple
of their rocky sides. A sloop was loitering in the distance, drop-
ping slowly down with the tide, her sail hanging uselessly
against the mast; and as the reflection of the sky gleamed along
the still water, it seemed as if the vessel was suspended in the air.

It was toward evening that Ichabod arrived at the castle of
the Herr Van Tassel, which he found thronged with the pride
and flower of the adjacent country. Old farmers, a spare
leathern-faced race, in homespun coats and breeches, blue
stockings, huge shoes, and magnificent pewter buckles. Their
brisk, withered little dames, in close crimped caps, long-waisted
gowns, homespun petticoats, with scissors and pin-cushions,
and gay calico pockets hanging on the outside. Buxom lasses,
almost as antiquated as their mothers, excepting where a straw
hat, a fine ribbon, or perhaps a white frock, gave symptoms

of city innovations. The sons, in short square skirted coats, with rows of stupendous brass buttons, and their hair generally queued in the fashion of the times, especially if they could procure an eelskin for the purpose, it being esteemed throughout the country as a potent nourisher and strengthener of the hair.

Brom Bones, however, was the hero of the scene, having come to the gathering on his favorite steed Daredevil, a creature, like himself, full of mettle and mischief, and which no one but himself could manage. He was, in fact, noted for preferring vicious animals, given to all kinds of tricks which kept the rider in constant risk of his neck, for he held a tractable, well-broken horse as unworthy of a lad of spirit.

Fain would I pause to dwell upon the world of charms that burst upon the enraptured gaze of my hero, as he entered the state parlor of Van Tassel's mansion. Not those of the bevy of buxom lasses, with their luxurious display of red and white; but the ample charms of a genuine Dutch country tea-table, in the sumptuous time of autumn. Such heaped-up platters of cakes of various and almost indescribable kinds, known only to experienced Dutch housewives! There was the doughty doughnut, the tender olykoek, and the crisp and crumbling cruller; sweet cakes and short cakes, ginger cakes and honey cakes, and the whole family of cakes. And then there were apple pies, and pumpkin pies; besides slices of ham and smoked beef; and moreover delectable dishes of preserved plums, and peaches, and pears, and quinces; not to mention broiled shad and roasted chickens; together with bowls of milk and cream, all mingled higgledy-piggledy, pretty much as I have enumerated them, with the motherly tea pot sending up its clouds of vapor from the midst — Heaven bless the mark! I want breath and time to discuss this banquet as it deserves, and am too eager to get on with my story. Happily, Ichabod Crane was not in so great a hurry as his historian, but did ample justice to every dainty.

He was a kind and thankful creature, whose heart dilated in proportion as his skin was filled with good cheer, and whose spirits rose with eating, as some men's do with drink. He could not help, too, rolling his large eyes round him as he ate, and chuckling with the possibility that he might one day be lord of all this scene of almost unimaginable luxury and splendor. Then, he thought, how soon he'd turn his back upon the old school-house; snap his fingers in the face of Hans Van Ripper, and every other niggardly patron, and kick any itinerant pedagogue out of doors that should dare to call him comrade!

Old Baltus Van Tassel moved about among his guests with a face dilated with content and good-humor, round and jolly as the harvest moon. His hospitable attentions were brief, but expressive, being confined to a shake of the hand, a slap on the shoulder, a loud laugh, and a pressing invitation to "fall to, and help themselves."

And now the sound of the music from the common room, or hall, summoned to the dance. The musician was an old gray-headed negro, who had been the itinerant orchestra of the neighborhood for more than half a century. His instrument was as old and battered as himself. The greater part of the time he scraped away on two or three strings, accompanying every movement of the bow with a motion of the head; bowing almost to the ground, and stamping with his foot whenever a fresh couple were to start.

Ichabod prided himself upon his dancing as much as upon his vocal powers. Not a limb, not a fibre about him was idle; and to have seen his loosely hung frame in full motion, and clattering about the room, you would have thought St. Vitus himself, that blessed patron of the dance, was figuring before you in person. He was the admiration of all the negroes; who, having gathered, of all ages and sizes, from the farm and the neighborhood, stood forming a pyramid of shining black faces at every door and window; gazing with delight at the scene; rolling their white eye-balls, and showing grinning rows of ivory from ear to ear. How could the flogger of urchins be otherwise than animated and joyous? the lady of his heart was his partner in the dance, and smiling graciously in reply to all his amorous oglings; while Brom Bones, sorely smitten with love and jealously, sat brooding by himself in one corner.

When the dance was at an end, Ichabod was attracted to a knot of the sager folks, who, with Old Van Tassel, sat smoking at one end of the piazza, gossiping over former times, and drawling out long stories about the war.

This neighborhood, at the time of which I am speaking, was one of those highly favored places which abound with chronicle and great men. The British and American line had run near it during the war; it had, therefore, been the scene of maurading, and infested with refugees, cow-boys, and all kind of border chivalry. Just sufficient time had elapsed to enable each story-teller to dress up his tale with a little becoming fiction, and, in the indistinctness of his recollection, to make himself the hero of every exploit.

There was the story of Doffue Martling, a large blue-bearded Dutchman, who had nearly taken a British frigate with an old iron nine-pounder from a mud breastwork, only that his gun burst at the sixth discharge. And there was an old gentleman who shall be nameless, being too rich a mynheer to be lightly mentioned, who in the battle of Whiteplains, being an excellent master of defence, parried a musket-ball with a small sword, insomuch that he absolutely felt it whiz round the blade, and glance off at the hilt; in proof of which he was ready at any time to show the sword, with the hilt a little bent. There were several more that had been equally great in the field, not one of whom but was persuaded that he had a considerable hand in bringing the war to a happy termination.

But all these were nothing to the tales of ghosts and apparitions that succeeded. The neighborhood is rich in legendary treasures of the kind. Local tales and superstitions thrive best in these sheltered, long-settled retreats; but are trampled under foot by the shifting throng that forms the population of most of our country places. Besides, there is no encouragement for ghosts in most of our villages, for they have scarcely had time to finsh their first nap, and turn themselves in their graves, before their surviving friends have travelled away from the neighborhood; so that when they turn out at night to walk their rounds, they have no acquaintance left to call upon. This is perhaps the reason why we so seldom hear of ghosts except in our long-established Dutch communities.

The immediate cause, however, of the prevalence of supernatural stories in these parts, was doubtless owing to the vicinity of Sleepy Hollow. There was a contagion in the very air that blew from that haunted region; it breathed forth an atmosphere of dreams and fancies infecting all the land. Several of the Sleepy Hollow people were present at the Van Tassel's, and, as usual, were doling out their wild and wonderful legends. Many dismal tales were told about funeral trains, and mourning cries and wailings heard and seen about the great tree where the unfortunate Major André was taken, and which stood in the neighborhood. Some mention was made also of the woman in white, that haunted the dark glen at Raven Rock, and was often heard to shriek on winter nights before a storm, having perished there in the snow. The chief part of the stories, however, turned upon the favorite spectre of Sleepy Hollow, the headless horseman, who had been heard several times of late, patrolling the country; and it is said, tethered his horse nightly among the graves in the churchyard.

The sequestered situation of this church seems always to have made it a favorite haunt of troubled spirits. It stands on a knoll, surrounded by locust-trees and lofty elms, from among which its decent, whitewashed walls shine modestly forth, like Christian purity, beaming through the shades of retirement. A gentle slope descends from it to a silver sheet of water, bordered by high trees, between which, peeps may be caught at the blue hills of the Hudson. To look upon its grass-grown yard, where the sunbeams seem to sleep so quietly, one would think that there at least the dead might rest in peace. On one side of the church extends a wide woody dell, along which raves a large brook among broken rocks and trunks of fallen trees. Over a deep black part of the stream, not far from the church, was formerly thrown a wooden bridge; the road that led to it, and the bridge itself, were thickly shaded by overhanging trees, which cast a gloom about it, even in the day-time; but occasioned a fearful darkness at night. Such was one of the favorite haunts of the headless horseman, and the place where he was most frequently encountered. The tale was told of old Brouwer, a most heretical disbeliever in ghosts, how he met the horseman returning from his foray into Sleepy Hollow, and was obliged to get up behind him; how they galloped over bush and brake, over hill and swamp, until they reached the bridge; when the horseman suddenly turned into a skeleton, threw old Brouwer into the brook, and sprang away over the tree-tops with a clap of thunder.

This story was immediately matched by a thrice marvellous adventure of Brom Bones, who made light of the galloping Hessian as an arrant jockey. He affirmed, that on returning one night from the neighboring village of Sing-Sing, he had been overtaken by a midnight trooper; that he had offered to race him for a bowl of punch, and should have won it too, for Daredevil beat the goblin horse all hollow, but just as they came to the church bridge, the Hessian bolted, and vanished in a flash of fire.

All these tales, told in that drowsy undertone with which men talk in the dark, the countenances of the listeners only now and then receiving a casual gleam from the glare of a pipe, sunk deep in the mind of Ichabod. He repaid them in kind with large extracts from his invaluable author, Cotton Mather, and added many marvellous events that had taken place in his native State of Connecticut, and fearful sights which he had seen in his nightly walks about Sleepy Hollow.

The revel now gradually broke up. The old farmers gathered together their families in their wagons, and were heard for some time rattling along the hollow roads, and over the distant hills. Some of the damsels mounted on pillions behind their favorite swains, and their light-hearted laughter mingling with the clattering of hoofs, echoed along the silent woodlands, sounding fainter and fainter, until they gradually died away — and the late scene of noise and frolic was all silent and deserted. Ichabod only lingered behind, according to the custom of country lovers, to have a tête-à-tête with the heiress; fully convinced that he was now on the high road to success. What passed at this interview I will not pretend to say, for in fact I do not know. Something, however, I fear me, must have gone wrong, for he certainly sallied forth, after no very great interval, with an air quite desolate and chapfallen — Oh, these women! these women! Could that girl have been playing off any of her coquettish tricks? — Was her encouragement of the poor pedagogue all a mere sham to secure her conquest of his rival? — Heaven only knows, not I! — Let it suffice to say, Ichabod stole forth with the air of one who had been sacking a henroost, rather than a fair lady's heart. Without looking to the right or left to notice the scene of rural wealth, on which he had so often gloated, he went straight to the stable, and with several hearty cuffs and kicks, roused his steed most uncourteously from the comfortable quarters in which he was soundly sleeping, dreaming of mountains of corn and oats, and whole valleys of timothy and clover.

It was the very witching hour of night that Ichabod, heavy-hearted, and crest-fallen, pursued his travel homewards, along the sides of the lofty hills which rise above Tarry Town, and which he had traversed so cheerily in the afternoon. The hour was as dismal as himself. Far below him the Tappan Zee spread its dusky and indistinct waste of waters, with here and there the tall mast of a sloop, riding quietly at anchor under the land. In the dead hush of midnight, he could even hear the barking of the watch-dog from the opposite shore of the Hudson; but it was so vague and faint as only to give an idea of his distance from this faithful companion of man. Now and then, too, the long-drawn crowing of a cock, accidentally awakened, would sound far, far off, from some farm-house away among the hills — but it was like a dreaming sound in his ear. No sign of life occurred near him, but occasionally the melancholy chirp of a cricket, or perhaps the guttural twang of a bull-frog from a neighboring marsh, as if sleeping uncomfortably, and turning suddenly in his bed.

All the stories of ghosts and goblins that he had heard in the afternoon, now came crowding upon his recollection. — The night grew darker and darker; the stars seemed to sink deeper in the sky, and driving clouds occasionally hid them from his sight. He had never felt so lonely and dismal. He was, moreover, approaching the very place where many of the scenes of the ghost stories had been laid. In the centre of the road stood an enormous tulip-tree, which towered like a giant above all the other trees of the neighborhood, and formed a kind of landmark. Its limbs were gnarled and fantastic, large enough to form trunks for ordinary trees, twisting down almost to the earth, and rising again into the air. It was connected with the tragical story of the unfortunate André, who had been taken prisoner hard by, and was universally known by the name of Major André's tree. The common people regarded it with a mixture of respect and superstition, partly out of sympathy for the fate of its ill-starred namesake, and partly from the tales of strange sights, and doleful lamentations, told concerning it.

As Ichabod approached this fearful tree, he began to whistle; he thought his whistle was answered: it was but a blast sweeping sharply through the dry branches. As he approached a little nearer, he thought he saw something white hanging in the midst of the tree: he paused, and ceased whistling; but on looking more narrowly, perceived that it was a place where the tree had been scathed by lightning, and the white wood laid bare. Suddenly he heard a groan — his teeth chattered, and his knees smote against the saddle: it was but the rubbing of one huge bough upon another, as they were swayed about by the breeze. He passed the tree in safety, but new perils lay before him.

About two hundred yards from the tree, a small brook crossed the road, and ran into a marshy and thickly-wooded glen, known by the name of Wiley's Swamp. A few rough logs laid side by side, served for a bridge over this stream. On that side of the road where the brook entered the wood, a group of oaks and chestnuts, matted thick with wild grape-vines, threw a cavernous gloom over it. To pass this bridge was the severest trial. It was at this identical spot that the unfortunate André was captured, and under the covert of those chestnuts and vines were the sturdy yeomen concealed who surprised him.

This has ever since been considered a haunted stream, and fearful are the feelings of a school-boy who has to pass it alone after dark.

As he approached the stream, his heart began to thump; he summoned up, however, all his resolution, gave his horse half a score of kicks in the ribs, and attempted to dash briskly across the bridge; but instead of starting forward, the perverse old animal made a lateral movement, and ran broadside against the fence. Ichabod, whose fears increased with the delay, jerked the reins on the other side, and kicked lustly with the contrary foot: it was all in vain; his steed started, it is true, but it was only to plunge to the opposite of the road into a thicket of brambles and alderbushes. The schoolmaster now bestowed both whip and heel upon the starveling ribs of old Gunpowder, who dashed forwards, snuffing and snorting, but came to a stand just by the bridge, with a suddenness that had nearly sent his rider sprawling over his head. Just at this moment a splashy tramp by the side of the bridge caught the sensitive ear of Ichabod. In the dark shadow of the grove, on the margin of the brook, he beheld something huge, mis-shapen, black and towering. It stirred not, but seemed gathered up in the gloom, like some gigantic monster ready to spring upon the traveller.

The hair of the affrighted pedagogue rose upon his head with terror. What was to be done? To turn and fly was now too late; and besides, what chance was there of escaping ghost or goblin, if such it was, which could ride upon the wings of the wind? Summoning up, therefore, a show of courage, he demanded in stammering accents—"Who are you?" He received no reply. He repeated his demand in a still more agitated voice. Still there was no answer. Once more he cudgelled the sides of the inflexible Gunpowder, and shutting his eyes, broke forth with involuntary fervor into a psalm tune. Just then the shadowy object of alarm put itself in motion, and with a scramble and a bound; stood at once in the middle of the road. Though the night was dark and dismal, yet the form of the unknown might now in some degree be ascertained. He appeared to be a horseman of large dimensions, and mounted on a black horse of powerful frame. He made no offer of molestation or sociability, but kept aloof on one side of the road, jogging along the blind side of old Gunpowder, who had now got over his fright and waywardness.

Ichabod, who had no relish for this strange midnight companion, and bethought himself of the adventure of Brom Bones with the galloping Hessian, now quickened his steed, in hopes of leaving him behind. The stranger, however, quickened his horse to an equal pace. Ichabod pulled up, and fell into a walk, thinking to lag behind—the other did the same. His heart began to sink within him; he endeavored to resume his psalm tune, but his parched tongue clove to the roof of his mouth, and he could not utter a stave. There was something in the moody and dogged silence of this pertinacious companion that was mysterious and appalling. It was soon fearfully accounted for. On mounting a rising ground, which brought the figure of his fellow-traveller in relief against the sky, gigantic in height, and muffled in a cloak, Ichabod was horror-struck, on perceiving that he was headless! but his horror was still more increased, on observing that the head, which should have rested on his shoulders, was carried before him on the pommel of his saddle! His terror rose to desperation; he rained a shower of kicks and blows upon Gunpowder, hoping, by a sudden movement, to give his companion the slip—but the spectre started full jump with him. Away, then, they dashed through thick and thin; stones flying and sparks flashing at every bound. Ichabod's flimsy garments fluttered in the air, as he stretched his long lank body away over his horse's head, in the eagerness of his flight.

They had now reached the road which turns off to Sleepy Hollow; but Gunpowder, who seemed possessed with a demon, instead of keeping up it, made an opposite turn, and plunged headlong down hill to the left. This road leads through a sandy hollow, shaded by trees for about a quarter of a mile, where it crosses the bridge famous in goblin story; and just beyond swells the green knoll on which stands the whitewashed church.

As yet the panic of the steed had given his unskillful rider an apparent advantage in the chase; but just as he had got half way through the hollow, the girths of the saddle gave way, and he felt it slipping from under him. He seized it by the pommel, and endeavored to hold it firm, but in vain; and had just time to save himself by clasping old Gunpowder round the neck, when the saddle fell to the earth, and he heard it trampled under foot by his pursuer. For a moment the terror of Hans Van Ripper's wrath passed across his mind — for it was his Sunday saddle; but this was no time for petty fears; the goblin was hard on his haunches; and (unskilled rider that he was!) he had much ado to maintain his seat; sometimes slipping on one side, sometimes on another, and sometimes jolted on the high ridge of his horse's backbone, with a violence that he verily feared would cleave him asunder.

An opening in the trees now cheered him with the hopes that the church bridge was at hand. The wavering reflection of a silver star in the bosom of the brook told him that he was not mistaken. He saw the walls of the church dimly glaring under the trees beyond. He recollected the place where Brom Bones' ghostly competitor had disappeared. "If I can but reach that bridge," thought Ichabod, "I am safe." Just then he heard the black steed panting and blowing close behind him; he even fancied that he felt his hot breath. Another convulsive kick in the ribs, and old Gunpowder sprung upon the bridge; he thundered over the resounding planks; he gained the opposite side, and now Ichabod cast a look behind to see if his pursuer should vanish, according to rule, in a flash of fire and brimstone. Just then he saw the goblin rising in his stirrups, and in the very act of hurling his head at him. Ichabod endeavored to dodge the horrible missile, but too late. It encountered his cranium with a tremendous crash — he was tumbled headlong into the dust, and Gunpowder, the black steed, and the goblin rider, passed by like a whirlwind.

The next morning the old horse was found without his saddle, and with the bridle under his feet, soberly cropping the grass at his master's gate. Ichabod did not make his appearance at breakfast — dinner-hour came, but no Ichabod. The boys assembled at the school-house, and strolled idly about the banks of the brook; but no schoolmaster. Hans Van Ripper now began to feel some uneasiness about the fate of poor Ichabod, and his saddle. An inquiry was set on foot, and after diligent investigation they came upon his traces. In one part of the road leading to the church, was found the saddle trampled in the dirt; the tracks of horses' hoofs deeply dented in the road, and, evidently at furious speed, were traced to the bridge, beyond which, on the bank of a broad part of the brook, where the water ran deep and black, was found the hat of the unfortunate Ichabod, and close beside it a shattered pumpkin.

The brook was searched, but the body of the schoolmaster was not to be discovered. Hans Van Ripper, as executor of his estate, examined the bundle which contained all his worldly effects. They consisted of two shirts and a half; two stocks for the neck; a pair or two of worsted stockings; an old pair of corduroy small-clothes; a rusty razor; a book of psalm tunes full of dog's ears; and a broken pitch-pipe. As to the books and furniture of the school-house, they belonged to the community, excepting Cotton Mather's History of Witchcraft, a New England Almanac, and a book of dreams and fortune-telling; in which last was a sheet of foolscap much scribbled and blotted, by several fruitless attempts to make a copy of verses in honor of the heiress of Van Tassel. These magic books and the poetic scrawl were forthwith consigned to the flames by Hans Van Ripper; who, from that time forward, determined to send his children no more to school; observing that he never knew any good come of this same reading and writing. Whatever money the schoolmaster possessed, and he had received his quarter's pay but a day or two before, he must have had about his person at the time of his disappearance.

The mysterious event caused much speculation at the church on the following Sunday. Knots of gazers and gossips were collected in the churchyard, at the bridge, and at the spot where the hat and pumpkin had been found. The stories of Brouwer, of Bones, and a whole budget of others, were called to mind; and when they had diligently considered them all, and compared them with the symptoms of the present case, they shook their heads, and came to the conclusion, that Ichabod had been carried off by the galloping Hessian. As he was a bachelor, and in nobody's debt, nobody troubled his head any more about him; the school was removed to a different quarter of the Hollow, and another pedagogue reigned in his stead.

It is true, an old farmer, who had been down to New York on a visit several years after, and from whom this account of the ghostly adventure was received, brought home the intelligence that Ichabod Crane was still alive; that he had left the neighborhood partly through fear of the goblin and Hans Van Ripper, and partly in mortification at having been suddenly dismissed by the heiress; that he had changed his quarters to a distant part of the country; had kept school and studied law at the same time; had been admitted to the bar; turned politician; electioneered; written for the newspapers; and finally, had been made a Justice of the Ten Pound Court. Brom Bones, too, who, shortly after his rival's disappearance, conducted the blooming Katrina in triumph to the altar, was observed to look exceedingly knowing whenever the story of Ichabod was related, and always burst into a hearty laugh at the mention of the pumpkin; which led some to suspect that he knew more about the matter than he chose to tell.

The old country wives, however, who are the best judges of these matters, maintain to this day that Ichabod was spirited away by supernatural means; and it is a favorite story often told about the neighborhood round the winter evening fire. The bridge became more than ever an object of superstitious awe; and that may be the reason why the road has been altered of late years, so as to approach the church by the border of the mill-pond. The school-house being deserted, soon fell to decay, and was reported to be haunted by the ghost of the unfortunate pedagogue; and the plough-boy, loitering homeward of a still summer evening, has often fancied his voice at a distance, chanting a melancholy psalm tune among the tranquil solitudes of Sleepy Hollow.

POSTSCRIPT,

Found in the Handwriting of Mr. Knickerbocker.

The preceding Tale is given, almost in the precise words in which I heard it related at a Corporation meeting of the ancient city of the Manhattoes,* at which were present many of its sagest and most illustrious burghers. The narrator was a pleasant, shabby, gentlemanly old fellow in pepper-and-salt clothes, with a sadly humorous face; and one whom I strongly suspected of being poor — he made such efforts to be entertaining. When his story was concluded there was much laughter and approbation, particularly from two or three deputy aldermen, who had been asleep the greater part of the time. There was, however, one tall, dry-looking old gentleman, with beetling eye-brows, who maintained a grave and rather severe face throughout; now and then folding his arms, inclining his head, and looking down upon the floor, as if turning a doubt over in his mind. He was one of your wary men, who never laugh but upon good grounds — when they have reason and the law on their side. When the mirth of the rest of the company had subsided, and silence was restored, he leaned one arm on the elbow of his chair, and sticking the other a-kimbo, demanded with a slight but exceedingly sage motion of the head, and contraction of the brow, what was the moral of the story, and what it went to prove.

The story-teller, who was just putting a glass of wine to his lips, as a refreshment after his toils, paused for a moment, looked at his inquirer with an air of infinite deference, and lowering the glass slowly to the table observed that the story was intended most logically to prove:

"That there is no situation in life but has its advantages and pleasures — provided we will but take a joke as we find it:

"That, therefore, he that runs races with goblin troopers, is likely to have rough riding of it:

"Ergo, for a country schoolmaster to be refused the hand

63

of a Dutch heiress, is a certain step to high preferment in the state."

The cautious old gentleman knit his brows tenfold closer after this explanation, being sorely puzzled by the ratiocination of the syllogism; while, methought, the one in pepper-and-salt eyed him with something of a triumphant leer. At length he observed that all of this was very well, but still he thought the story a little on the extravagant — there were one or two points on which he had his doubts.

"Faith, sir," replied the story-teller, "as to that matter, I don't believe one-half of it myself."

D. K.

*New York

RIP VAN WINKLE

A Posthumous Writing of
Diedrich Knickerbocker

By Woden, God of Saxons,
From whence comes Wensday, that is Wodnesday.
Truth is a thing that ever I will keep
Unto thylke day in which I creep into
My sepulchre —

Cartright.

WHOEVER HAS MADE a voyage up the Hudson, must remember the Kaatskill mountains. They are a dismembered branch of the great Appalachian family, and are seen away to the west of the river, swelling up to a noble height, and lording it over the surrounding country. Every change of season, every change of weather, indeed every hour of the day produces some change in the magical hues and shapes of these mountains; and they are regarded by all the good wives, far and near, as perfect barometers. When the weather is fair and settled, they are clothed in blue and purple, and print their bold outlines on the clear evening sky; but sometimes, when the rest of the landscape is cloudless, they will gather a hood of gray vapors about their summits, which, in the last rays of the setting sun, will glow and light up like a crown of glory.

At the foot of these fairy mountains, the voyager may have descried the light smoke curling up from a village, whose shingle roofs gleam among the trees, just where the blue tints of the upland melt away into the fresh green of the nearer landscape. It is a little village of great antiquity, having been

65

founded by some of the Dutch colonists, in the early times of the province, just about the beginning of the government of the good Peter Stuyvesant (may he rest in peace!) and there were some of the houses of the original settlers standing within a few years, built of small yellow bricks, brought from Holland, having latticed windows and gable fronts, surmounted with weathercocks.

In that same village, and in one of these very houses (which to tell the precise truth, was sadly time-worn and weather-beaten), there lived many years since, while the country was yet a province of Great Britain, a simple, good-natured fellow, of the name of Rip Van Winkle. He was a descendant of the Van Winkles who figured so gallantly in the chivalrous days of Peter Stuyvesant, and accompanied him to the siege of fort Christina. He inherited, however, but little of the martial character of his ancestors. I have observed that he was a simple good-natured man; he was moreover a kind neighbor, and an obedient henpecked husband. Indeed, to the latter circumstance might be owing that meekness of spirit which gained him such universal popularity; for those men are most apt to be obsequious and conciliating abroad, who are under the discipline of shrews at home. Their tempers, doubtless, are rendered pliant and malleable in the fiery furnace of domestic tribulation, and a curtain lecture is worth all the sermons in the world for teaching the virtues of patience and long-suffering. A termagant wife may, therefore, in some respects, be considered a tolerable blessing; and if so, Rip Van Winkle was thrice blessed.

Certain it is that he was a great favorite among all the good wives of the village, who, as usual with the amiable sex, took his part in all family squabbles, and never failed, whenever they talked those matters over in their evening gossipings, to lay all the blame on Dame Van Winkle. The children of the village, too, would shout with joy whenever he approached. He assisted at their sports, made their playthings, taught them to fly kites and shoot marbles, and told them long stories of ghosts, witches, and Indians. Whenever he went dodging about the village, he was surrounded by a troop of them hanging on his skirts, clambering on his back, and playing a thousand tricks on him with impunity; and not a dog would bark at him throughout the neighborhood.

The great error in Rip's composition was an insuperable aversion to all kinds of profitable labor. It could not be from the want of assiduity or perseverance; for he would sit on a wet rock, with a rod as long and heavy as a Tartar's lance, and fish all day without a murmur, even though he should not be encouraged by a single nibble. He would carry a fowling-piece on his shoulder, for hours together, trudging through woods and swamps, and up hill and down dale, to shoot a few squirrels or wild pigeons. He would never refuse to assist a neighbor even in the roughest toil, and was a foremost man at all country frolics for husking Indian corn, or building stone fences. The women of the village, too, used to employ him to run their errands, and to do such little odd jobs as their less obliging husbands would not do for them; — in a word, Rip was ready to attend to anybody's business but his own; but as to doing family duty, and keeping his farm in order, he found it impossible.

In fact, he declared it was of no use to work on his farm; it was the most pestilent little piece of ground in the whole country; everything about it went wrong, and would go wrong in spite of him. His fences were continually falling to pieces; his cow would either go astray, or get among the cabbages; weeds were sure to grow quicker in his fields than anywhere else; the rain always made a point of setting in just as he had some out-door work to do; so that though his patrimonial estate had dwindled away under his management, acre by acre, until there was little more left than a mere patch of Indian corn and potatoes, yet it was the worst conditioned farm in the neighborhood.

His children, too, were as ragged and wild as if they belonged to nobody. His son Rip, an urchin begotten in his own likeness, promised to inherit the habits, with the old clothes of his father. He was generally seen trooping like a colt at his mother's heels, equipped in a pair of his father's cast-off galligaskins, which he had much ado to hold up with one hand, as a fine lady does her train in bad weather.

Rip Van Winkle, however, was one of those happy mortals, of foolish, well-oiled dispositions, who take the world easy, eat white bread or brown, whichever can be got with least thought or trouble, and would rather starve on a penny than work for a pound. If left to himself, he would have whistled life away, in perfect contentment; but his wife kept continually dinning in his ears about his idleness, his carelessness, and the ruin he was bringing on his family.

Morning, noon, and night, her tongue was incessantly going, and everything he said or did was sure to produce a torrent of household eloquence. Rip had but one way of replying to all lectures of the kind, and that, by frequent use, had grown into a habit. He shrugged his shoulders, shook his head, cast up his eyes, but said nothing. This, however, always provoked a fresh volley from his wife, so that he was fain to draw off his forces, and take to the outside of the house—the only side which, in truth, belongs to a henpecked husband.

Rip's sole domestic adherent was his dog Wolf, who was as much henpecked as his master; for Dame Van Winkle regarded them as companions in idleness, and even looked upon Wolf with an evil eye, as the cause of the master's going so often astray. True it is, in all points of spirit befitting an honorable dog, he was as courageous an animal as ever scoured the woods—but what courage can withstand the ever-during and all besetting terrors of a woman's tongue? The moment Wolf entered the house, his crest fell, his tail drooped to the ground, or curled between his legs, he sneaked about with a gallows air, casting many a sidelong glance at Dame Van Winkle, and at the least flourish of a broomstick or ladle, he would fly to the door with yelping precipitation.

Times grew worse and worse with Rip Van Winkle, as years of matrimony rolled on: a tart temper never mellows with age, and a sharp tongue is the only edge tool that grows keener with constant use. For a long while he used to console himself, when driven from home, by frequenting a kind of perpetual club of the sages, philosophers, and other idle personages of the village, which held its sessions on a bench before a small inn, designated by a rubicund portrait of his majesty George the Third. Here they used to sit in the shade of a long lazy summer's day, talking listlessly over village gossip, or telling endless sleepy stories about nothing. But it would have been worth any statesman's money to have heard the profound discussions which sometimes took place, when by chance an old newspaper fell into their hands, from some passing traveller. How solemnly they would listen to the contents, as drawled out by Derrick Van Bummel, the schoolmaster, a dapper learned little man, who was not to be daunted by the most gigantic word in the dictionary; and how sagely they would deliberate upon public events some months after they had taken place.

The opinions of this junto were completely controlled by Nicholas Vedder, a patriarch of the village, and landlord of the inn, at the door of which he took his seat from morning till night, just moving sufficiently to avoid the sun, and keep in the shade of a large tree; so that the neighbors could tell the hour by his movements as accurately as by a sun-dial. It is true, he was rarely heard to speak, but smoked his pipe incessantly. His adherents, however (for every great man has his adherents), perfectly understood him, and knew how to gather his opinions. When anything that was read or related displeased him, he was observed to smoke his pipe vehemently, and to send forth short, frequent, and angry puffs; but when pleased, he would inhale the smoke slowly and tranquilly, and emit it in light and placid clouds, and sometimes taking the pipe from his mouth, and letting the fragrant vapor curl about his nose, would gravely nod his head in token of perfect approbation.

From even this stronghold the unlucky Rip was at length routed by his termagant wife, who would suddenly break in upon the tranquillity of the assemblage, and call the members all to nought; nor was that august personage, Nicholas Vedder himself, sacred from the daring tongue of this terrible virago, who charged him outright with encouraging her husband in habits of idleness.

Poor Rip was at last reduced almost to despair, and his only alternative to escape from the labor of the farm and the clamor of his wife, was to take gun in hand, and stroll away into the woods. Here he would sometimes seat himself at the foot of a tree, and share the contents of his wallet with Wolf, with whom he sympathized as a fellow-sufferer in persecution. "Poor Wolf," he would say, "thy mistress leads thee a dog's life of it; but never mind, my lad, whilst I live thou shalt never want a friend to stand by thee!" Wolf would wag his tail, look wistfully in his master's face, and if dogs can feel pity, I verily believe he reciprocated the sentiment with all his heart.

In a long ramble of the kind, on a fine autumnal day, Rip had unconciously scrambled to one of the highest parts of the Kaatskill mountains. He was after his favorite sport of squirrel-shooting, and the still solitudes had echoed and re-echoed with the reports of his gun. Panting and fatigued, he threw himself, late in the afternoon, on a green knoll covered with mountain herbage, that crowned the brow of a precipice. From an opening between the trees, he could overlook all the lower country for many a mile of rich woodland. He saw at a distance the lordly Hudson, far, far below him, moving on its silent but majestic course, with the reflection of a purple cloud, or the sail of a lagging bark, here and there sleeping on its glassy bosom, and at last losing itself in the blue highlands.

On the other side he looked down into a deep mountain glen, wild, lonely, and shagged, the bottom filled with fragments from the impending cliffs, and scarcely lighted by the reflected rays of the setting sun. For some time Rip lay musing on this scene; evening was gradually advancing; the mountains began to throw their long blue shadows over the valleys; he saw that it would be dark long before he could reach the village; and he heaved a heavy sigh when he thought of encountering the terrors of Dame Van Winkle.

As he was about to descend he heard a voice from a distance hallooing, "Rip Van Winkle! Rip Van Winkle!" He looked around, but could see nothing but a crow winging its solitary flight across the mountain. He thought his fancy must have deceived him, and turned again to descend, when he heard the same cry ring through the still evening air, "Rip Van Winkle! Rip Van Winkle!" — at the same time Wolf bristled up his back, and giving a low growl, skulked to his master's side, looking fearfully down into the glen. Rip now felt a vague apprehension stealing over him; he looked anxiously in the same direction, and perceived a strange figure slowly toiling up the rocks, and bending under the weight of something he carried on his back. He was surprised to see any human being in this lonely and unfrequented place, but supposing it to be some one of the neighborhood in need of his assistance, he hastened down to yield it.

On nearer approach, he was still more surprised at the singularity of the stranger's appearance. He was a short square-built old fellow, with thick bushy hair, and a grizzled beard. His dress was of the antique Dutch fashion — a cloth jerkin strapped round the waist — several pair of breeches, the outer one of ample volume, decorated with rows of buttons down the sides, and bunches at the knees. He bore on his shoulders a stout keg, that seemed full of liquor, and made signs for Rip to approach and assist him with the load. Though rather shy and distrustful of this new acquaintance, Rip complied with his usual alacrity, and mutually relieving each other, they clambered up a narrow gully, apparently the dry bed of a mountain torrent. As they ascended, Rip every now and then heard long rolling peals, like distant thunder, that seemed to issue out of a deep ravine, or rather cleft between lofty rocks, toward which their rugged path conducted. He paused for an instant, but supposing it to be the muttering of one of those transient thunder showers which often take place in the mountain heights, he proceeded. Passing through the ravine, they came to a hollow, like a small amphitheatre, surrounded by perpendicular precipices, over the brinks of which, impending trees shot their branches so that you only caught glimpses of the azure sky, and the bright evening cloud. During the whole time, Rip and his companion had labored on in silence; for though the former marvelled greatly what could be the object of carrying a keg of liquor up this wild mountain, yet there was something strange and incomprehensible about the unknown, that inspired awe, and checked familiarity.

On entering the amphitheatre, new objects of wonder presented themselves. On a level spot in the centre was a company of odd-looking personages playing at nine-pins. They were dressed in a quaint outlandish fashion: some wore short doublets, others jerkins, with long knives in their belts, and most of them had enormous breeches, of similar style with that of the guide's. Their visages too, were peculiar: one had a large head, broad face, and small piggish eyes; the face of another seemed to consist entirely of nose, and was surmounted by a white sugar-loaf hat, set off with a little red cock's tail. They all had beards, of various shapes and colors. There was one who seemed to be the commander. He was a stout old gentleman, with a weather-beaten countenance; he wore a laced doublet, broad belt and hanger, high-crowned hat and feather, red stockings, and high-heeled shoes, with roses in them. The whole group reminded Rip of the figures in an old Flemish painting, in the parlor of Dominie Van Schaick, the village parson, and which had been brought over from Holland at the time of the settlement.

What seemed particularly odd to Rip was, that though these folks were evidently amusing themselves, yet they maintained the gravest faces, the most mysterious silence, and were, withal, the most melancholy party of pleasure he had ever witnessed. Nothing interrupted the stillness of the scene but the noise of the balls, which, whenever they were rolled, echoed along the mountains like rumbling peals of thunder.

As Rip and his companion approached them, they suddenly desisted from their play, and stared at him with such a fixed statue-like gaze, and such strange, uncouth, lack-lustre countenances, that his heart turned within him, and his knees smote together. His companion now emptied the contents of the keg into large flagons, and made signs to him to wait upon the company. He obeyed with fear and trembling; they quaffed the liquor in profound silence, and then returned to their game.

By degrees, Rip's awe and apprehension subsided. He even ventured, when no eye was fixed upon him, to taste the beverage, which he found had much the flavor of excellent Hollands. He was naturally a thirsty soul, and was soon tempted to repeat the draught. One taste provoked another, and he reiterated his visits to the flagon so often, that at length his senses were overpowered, his eyes swam in his head, his head gradually declined, and he fell into a deep sleep.

On waking, he found himself on the green knoll from whence he had first seen the old man of the glen. He rubbed his eyes — it was a bright sunny morning. The birds were hopping and twittering among the bushes, and the eagle was wheeling aloft, and breasting the pure mountain breeze. "Surely," thought Rip, "I have not slept here all night." He recalled the occurrences before he fell asleep. The strange man with the keg of liquor — the mountain ravine — the wild retreat among the rocks — the wo-begone party at nine-pins — the flagon — "Oh! that wicked flagon!" thought Rip — "what excuse shall I make to Dame Van Winkle?"

He looked round for his gun, but in place of the clean, well-oiled fowling-piece, he found an old firelock lying by him, the barrel encrusted with rust, the lock falling off, and the stock worm-eaten. He now suspected that the grave roysterers of the mountain had put a trick upon him, and having dosed him with liquor, robbed him of his gun. Wolf, too, had disappeared, but he might have strayed away after a squirrel or partridge. He whistled after him and shouted his name, but all in vain; the echoes repeated his whistle and shout, but no dog was to be seen.

He determined to revisit the scene of the last evening's gambol, and if he met with any of the party, to demand his dog and gun. As he rose to walk, he found himself stiff in the joints, and wanting in his usual activity. "These mountain beds do not agree with me," thought Rip, "and if this frolic should lay me up with a fit of the rheumatism, I shall have a blessed time with Dame Van Winkle." With some difficulty he got down into the glen; he found the gully up which he and his companion had ascended the preceding evening; but to his astonishment a mountain stream was now foaming down it, leaping from rock to rock, and filling the glen with babbling murmurs. He, however, made shift to scramble up its sides, working his toilsome way through thickets of birch, sassafras, and witchhazel; and sometimes tripped up or entangled by the wild grape vines that twisted their coils and tendrils from tree to tree, and spread a kind of network in his path.

At length he reached to where the ravine had opened through the cliffs to the amphitheatre; but no traces of such opening remained. The rocks presented a high impenetrable wall, over which the torrent came tumbling in a sheet of feathery foam, and fell into a broad, deep basin, black from the shadows of the surrounding forest. Here, then, poor Rip was brought to a stand. He again called and whistled after his dog; he was only answered by the cawing of a flock of idle crows, sporting high in the air about a dry tree that overhung a sunny precipice; and who, secure in their elevation, seemed to look down and scoff at the poor man's perplexities. What was to be done? The morning was passing away, and Rip felt famished for want of his breakfast. He grieved to give up his dog and gun; he dreaded to meet his wife; but it would not do to starve among the mountains. He shook his head, shouldered the rusty firelock, and with a heart full of trouble and anxiety, turned his steps homeward.

As he approached the village, he met a number of people, but none whom he knew, which somewhat surprised him, for he had thought himself acquainted with every one in the country round. Their dress, too, was of a different fashion from that to which he was accustomed. They all stared at him with equal marks of surprise, and whenever they cast eyes upon him, invariably stroked their chins. The constant recurrence of this gesture induced Rip, involuntarily, to do the same, when, to his astonishment, he found his beard had grown a foot long!

He had now entered the skirts of the village. A troop of strange children ran at his heels, hooting after him, and pointing at his grey beard. The dogs, too, not one of which he recognized for an old acquaintance, barked at him as he passed. The very village was altered: it was larger and more populous. There were rows of houses which he had never seen before, and those which had been his familiar haunts had disappeared. Strange names were over the doors — strange faces at the windows — everything was strange. His mind now misgave him; he began to doubt whether both he and the world around him were not bewitched. Surely this was his native village, which he had left but a day before. There stood the Kaatskill mountains — there ran the silver Hudson at a distance — there was every hill and dale precisely as it had always been — Rip was sorely perplexed — "That flagon last night," thought he, "has addled my poor head sadly!"

It was with some difficulty that he found his way to his own house, which he approached with silent awe, expecting every moment to hear the shrill voice of Dame Van Winkle. He found the house gone to decay — the roof fallen in, the windows shattered, and the doors off the hinges. A half-starved dog, that looked like Wolf, was skulking about it. Rip called him by name, but the cur snarled, showed his teeth, and passed on. This was an unkind cut indeed. — "My very dog," sighed poor Rip, "has forgotton me!"

He entered the house, which, to tell the truth, Dame Van Winkle had always kept in neat order. It was empty, forlorn, and apparently abandoned. This desolateness overcame all his connubial fears — he called loudly for his wife and children — the lonely chambers rang for a moment with his voice, and then all again was silence.

He now hurried forth, and hastended to his old resort, the village inn — but it too was gone. A large rickety wooden building stood in its place, with great gaping windows, some of them broken, and mended with old hats and petticoats, and over the door was painted, "The Union Hotel, by Jonathan Doolittle." Instead of the great tree that used to shelter the quiet little Dutch inn of yore, there now was reared a tall naked pole, with something on the top that looked like a red nightcap, and from it was fluttering a flag, on which was a singular assemblage of stars and strips — all this was strange and incomprehensible. He recognized on the sign, however, the ruby face of King George, under which he had smoked so many a peaceful pipe, but even this was singularly metamorphosed. The red coat was changed for one of blue and buff, a sword was held in the hand instead of a sceptre, the head was decorated with a cocked hat, and underneath was painted in large characters, GENERAL WASHINGTON.

There was, as usual, a crowd of folk about the door, but none that Rip recollected. The very character of the people seemed changed. There was a busy, bustling, disputatious tone about it, instead of the accustomed phlegm and drowsy tranquility. He looked in vain for sage Nicholas Vedder, with his broad face, double chin, and fair long pipe, uttering clouds of tobacco smoke, instead of idle speeches; or Van Bummel, the schoolmaster, doling forth the contents of an ancient newspaper. In place of these, a lean bilious-looking fellow, with his pockets full of handbills, was haranguing vehemently about rights of citizens — election — members of Congress — liberty — Bunker's hill — heroes of seventy-six — and other words, that was a perfect Babylonish jargon to the bewildered Van Winkle.

The appearance of Rip, with his long, grizzled beard, his rusty fowling-piece, his uncouth dress, and the army of women and children that had gathered at his heels, soon attracted the attention of the tavern politicians. They crowded round him, eyed him from head to foot, with great curiosity. The orator bustled up to him, and drawing him partly aside, inquired, "on which side he voted?" Rip stared in vacant stupidity. Another short but busy little fellow pulled him by the arm, and rising on tiptoe, inquired in his ear, "whether he was Federal or Democrat." Rip was equally at a loss to comprehend the question; when a knowing, self-important old gentleman, in a sharp cocked hat, made his way through the crowd, putting them to the right and left with his elbows as he passed, and planting himself before Van Winkle, with one arm a-

kimbo, the other resting on his cane, his keen eyes and sharp
hat penetrating, as it were, into his very soul, demanded in
an austere tone, "what brought him to the election with a gun
on his shoulder, and a mob at his heels, and whether he meant ,
to breed a riot in the village?"

"Alas! gentlemen," cried Rip, somewhat dismayed, "I am
a poor, quiet man, a native of the place, and a loyal subject
of the King, God bless him!"

Here a general shout burst from the bystanders—"a tory!
a tory! a spy! a refugee! hustle him! away with him!"

It was with great difficulty that the self-important man in
the cocked hat restored order; and having assumed a tenfold
austerity of brow, demanded again of the unknown culprit,
what he came there for, and whom he was seeking. The poor
man humbly assured him that he meant no harm, but merely
came there in search of some of his neighbors, who used too
keep about the tavern.

"Well—who are they?—name them."

Rip bethought himself a moment, and inquired, "Where's
Nicholas Vedder?"

There was a silence for a little while, when an old man
replied, in a thin, piping voice, "Nicholas Vedder? why, he
is dead and gone these eighteen years! There was a wooden
tomb-stone in the church-yard that used to tell all about him,
but that's rotten and gone too."

"Where's Brom Dutcher?"

"Oh, he went off to the army in the beginning of the war;
some say he was killed at the storming of Stony-Point—others
say he was drowned in the squall, at the foot of Antony's Nose.
I don't know—he never came back again."

"Where's Van Bummel, the schoolmaster?"

"He went off to the wars, too; was a great militia general,
and is not in Congress."

Rip's heart died away, at hearing of these sad changes in
his home and friends, and finding himself thus alone in the
world. Every answer puzzled him, too, by treating of such enormous lapses of time, and of matters which he could not unders-

tand: war — Congress — Stony-Point — he had no courage to ask after any more friends, but cried out in despair, "Does nobody here know Rip Van Winkle?"

"Oh, Rip Van Winkle!" exclaimed two or three. "Oh, to be sure! that's Rip Van Winkle yonder, leaning against the tree."

Rip looked, and beheld a precise counterpart of himself as he went up the mountain; apparently as lazy, and certainly as ragged. The poor fellow was now completely confounded. He doubted his own identity, and whether he was himself or another man. In the midst of his bewilderment, the man in the cocked hat demanded who he was, and what was his name?

"God knows," exclaimed he at his wit's end; "I'm not myself — I'm somebody else — that's me yonder — no — that's somebody else, got into my shoes — I was myself last night, but I fell asleep on the mountain, and they've changed my gun, and everything's changed, and I'm changed, and I can't tell what's my name, or who I am!"

The by-standers began now to look at each other, nod, wink significantly, and tap their fingers against their foreheads. There was a whisper, also, about securing the gun, and keeping the old fellow from doing mischief; at the very suggestion of which, the self-important man with the cocked hat retired with some precipitation. At this critical moment a fresh comely woman passed through the throng to get a peep at the gray-bearded man. She had a chubby child in her arms, which, frightened at his looks, began to cry. "Hush, Rip," cried she, "hush you little fool; the old man won't hurt you." The name of the child, the air of the mother, the tone of her voice, all awakened a train of recollections in his mind.

"What is your name, my good woman?" asked he.

"Judith Gardenier."

"And your father's name?"

"Ah, poor man, his name was Rip Van Winkle; it's twenty years since he went away from home with his gun, and never has been heard of since — his dog came home without him; but whether he shot himself, or was carried away by the Indians, nobody can tell. I was then but a little girl."

Rip had but one question more to ask; but he put it with a faltering voice:

"Where's your mother?"

Oh, she too had died but a short time since: she broke a blood-vessel in a fit of passion at a New-England pedler.

There was a drop of comfort, at least, in this intelligence. The honest man could contain himself no longer. He caught his daughter and her child in his arms. "I am your father!" cried he—"Young Rip Van Winkle once—old Rip Van Winkle now—Does nobody know poor Rip Van Winkle!"

All stood amazed, until an old woman, tottering out from among the crowd, put her hand to her brow, and peering under it in his face for a moment, exclaimed. "Sure enough! it is Rip Van Winkle—it is himself. Welcome home again, old neighbor—Why, where have you been these twenty long years?"

Rip's story was soon told, for the whole twenty years had been to him but as one night. The neighbors stared when they heard it; some were seen to wink at each other, and put their tongues in their cheeks; and the self-important man in the cocked hat, who, when the alarm was over, had returned to the field, screwed down the corners of his mouth, and shook his head—upon which there was a general shaking of the head throughout the assemblage.

It was determined, however, to take the opinion of old Peter Vanderdonk, who was seen slowly advancing up the road. He was a descendant of the historian of that name, who wrote one of the earliest accounts of the province. Peter was the most ancient inhabitant of the village, and well versed in all the wonderful events and traditions of the neighborhood. He recollected Rip at once, and corroborated his story in the most satisfactory manner. He assured the company that it was a fact, handed down from his ancestor the historian, that the Kaatskill mountains had always been haunted by strange beings. That it was affirmed that the great Hendrick Hudson, the first discoverer of the river and country, kept a kind of vigil there every twenty years, with his crew of the Half-moon, being permitted in this way to revisit the scenes of his enterprise, and keep a guardian eye upon the river and the great city called by his name. That his father had once seen them in their old Dutch dresses playing at nine-pins in the hollow of the mountain; and that he himself had heard, one summer afternoon, the sound of their balls, like distant peals of thunder.

To make a long story short, the company broke up and returned to the more important concerns of the election. Rip's daughter took him home to live with her; she had a snug, well-furnished house, and a stout cheery farmer for a husband, whom Rip recollected for one of the urchins that used to climb upon his back. As to Rip's son and heir, who was the ditto of himself, seen leaning against the tree, he was employed to work on the farm, but evinced a hereditary disposition to attend to anything else but his business.

Rip now resumed his old walks and habits; he soon found many of his former cronies, though all rather the worse for the wear and tear of time; and preferred making friends among the rising generation, with whom he soon grew into great favor.

Having nothing to do at home, and being arrived at that happy age when a man can do nothing with impunity, he took his place once more on the bench, at the inn door, and was reverenced as one of the patriarchs of the village, and a chronicle of the old times "before the war." It was some time before he could get into the regular track of gossip, or could be made to comprehend the strange events that had taken place during his torpor. How that there had been a revolutionary war — that the country had thrown off the yoke of old England — and that, instead of being a subject of his majesty George the Third, he was now a free citizen of the United States. Rip, in fact, was no politician; the changes of states and empires made but little impression on him; but there was one species of despotism under which he had long groaned, and that was — petticoat government. Happily that was at an end; he had got his neck out of the yoke of matrimony, and could go in and out whenever he pleased, without dreading the tyranny of Dame Van Winkle. Whenever her name was mentioned, however, he shook his head, shrugged his shoulders, and cast up his eyes; which might pass either for an expression of resignation to his fate, or joy at his deliverance.

He used to tell his story to every stranger that arrived at Mr. Doolittle's hotel. He was observed, at first, to vary on some points every time he told it, which was doubtless owing to his having so recently awaked. It at last settled down precisely to the tale I have related, and not a man, woman, or child in the neighborhood, but knew it by heart. Some always pretended to doubt the reality of it, and insisted that Rip had been out of his head, and that this was one point on which he always remained flighty. The old Dutch inhabitants, however, almost universally gave it full credit. Even to this day, they never hear a thunder-storm of a summer afternoon about the Kaatskill, but they say Hendrick Hudson and his crew are at their game of nine-pins; and it is a common wish of all henpecked husbands in the neighborhood, when life hangs heavy on their hands, that they might have a quieting draft out of Rip Van Winkle's flagon.

NOTE. — The foregoing tale, one would suspect, had been suggested to Mr. Knickerbocker by a little German superstition about the Emperor Frederick *der Rothbart* and the Kypphauser mountain; the subjoined note, however, which he had appended to the tale, shows that it is an absolute fact, narrated with his usual fidelity.

"The story of Rip Van Winkle may seem incredible to many, but nevertheless I give it my full belief, for I know the vicinity of our old Dutch settlements to have been very subject to marvellous events and appearances. Indeed, I have heard many stranger stories than this, in the villages along the Hudson; all of which were too well authenticated to admit of a doubt. I have even talked with Rip Van Winkle myself, who, when I last saw him, was a very venerable old man, and so perfectly rational and consistent on every other point, that I think no conscientious person could refuse to take this into the bargain; nay, I have seen a certificate on the subject taken before a country justice, and signed with a cross, in the justice's own hand writing. The story, therefore, is beyond the possibility of doubt."

LEARNING INCORPORATED is a non-profit organization devoted to the improvement of education. Profits to Learning Incorporated from the sale of this book go to its scholarship and public service fund. The scholarship program assists people with learning handicaps who lack money to pay for help.

Ther nesvt th childen

written by a person age 12, grade 7, and IQ 130

Do you know what he MEANT?
Could the message be a matter of LIFE or DEATH?

OVERCOME LEARNING HANDICAPS

Everyone has learning handicaps of some sort. Learning to communicate effectively is a major problem with most people. The learning handicap, dyslexia, caused Edison, Einstein, Wilson, and other intelligent people much anguish when learning to read and spell. Poor visual perception can cause people, whose eyes have 20-20 or better sight, to think they see things they don't really see. Poor visual memory causes people not to remember accurately things they've seen. Learning Incorporated works to help people overcome learning handicaps such as these.

IMPROVE LEARNING SKILLS

Many people never fully develop their learning potential to peak capacity. They go through life like a car with eight cylinders using only a few cylinders.

LEARNING INCORPORATED
Manset, Maine 04656

Also published by LEARNING INCORPORATED:

GUIDE
to
learning . . .

Experts say everyone has variations of learning handicaps, but those who can identify and work at overcoming them prosper better. Your handiest and one-of-a-kind guide to identify and thereby overcome these is

THE LEARNING INCORPORATED
DICTIONARY OF LEARNING HANDICAPS.

It is an alphabetically arranged 16 page (4 x 8½" to be easily kept in a pocket for quick reference) paperback list. And, the professional *Journal of Learning Disabilities* says, " . . . it is worthwhile. It offers brief but precise and sensible definitions of many of the terms and concepts likely to be encountered in the field of learning handicaps." Knowledge from it will improve your communications. For each ordered send $1.00 to Learning Inc., Manset, Maine 04656. Groups wishing to distribute these as a public service to parents, teachers and/or others in their community can get a discount.

This is to certify that I have known Stillwell Esq.
of Kinderhook for about ⅔ of a century & believe
him to be a man of honor & integrity & is the same
person celebrated in the writings of the Old world
— something under the Creation of Ichabod Crane
in his famous Legend of Sleepy Hollow

M Van Buren

Kinderhook May 16, 1846.

The Van Buren Certificate